FIGHTING FOR YOUR PURPOSE

Fighting for Your Purpose: From Sex Trafficking to Ministry

Copyright © 2020 by Sula Skiles

All rights reserved solely by the author. The author guarantees all contents are original and do not infringe upon the legal rights of any other person or work. No part of this book may be reproduced in any form without the permission of the author. The views expressed in this book are not necessarily those of the publisher.

Scripture taken from the New King James Version®. Copyright © 1982 by Thomas Nelson. Used by permission. All rights reserved.

Scripture quotations marked TPT are from The Passion Translation®. Copyright © 2017, 2018 by Passion & Fire Ministries, Inc. Used by permission. All rights reserved. ThePassionTranslation.com.

Scripture quotations from The Authorized (King James) Version. Rights in the Authorized Version in the United Kingdom are vested in the Crown. Reproduced by permission of the Crown's patentee, Cambridge University Press

Scripture quotations taken from the Amplified® Bible (AMP), Copyright © 2015 by The Lockman Foundation Used by permission. www.Lockman.org

ISBN-13: 9798632985147

A Publication of Tall Pine Books | *where your purpose meets print* || tallpinebooks.com

FIGHTING FOR YOUR PURPOSE

FROM SEX TRAFFICKING TO MINISTRY

SULA SKILES

Tall Pine

CONTENTS

PART ONE
1. 1.0 Glimpses of My Traumatic Life — 3

PART TWO
2. 2.1 The Basics — 33
3. 2.2 The Transformation — 45
4. 2.3 The Recovery — 61
5. 2.4 The "Yes" — 77
6. 2.5 The Supernatural Help — 91
7. 2.6 The Gifts — 103
8. 2.7 The Delay — 119
9. 2.8 The Fight — 131
10. 2.9 The Prep Time — 143
11. 2.10 The Alignment — 151
12. 2.11 The Dream — 159

Additional Resources — 169
Meet the Author — 179

PART ONE_

1.0 GLIMPSES OF MY TRAUMATIC LIFE_

My earliest memories in life are of sexual abuse. I remember being pushed under heavy comforters, large mouths covering my little toddler lips, large body parts violating my little body parts, and being suffocated. It was so hard to breathe. I would scream inside, but nothing came out. I had so much fear because I remember someone threatening me not to tell, or else. This treatment was my "normal." I don't remember anything before that. I was 18 months old when sexual violation and abuse started. It was only the beginning of a lifetime of horrible events sewn together like a patchwork quilt depicting a dark, traumatic nightmare almost too terrible to be true.

My mom was a very hard-working young woman. She had me at age 19 and was determined to be successful in life. She was in school preparing for her master's degree and doing the best that she could as a single mom. My sexual abuse occurred while being watched by a trusted couple who were friends and had a daughter a year-and-a-half older than me. One day, my mom was tickling me and did a raspberry on my belly, making that funny sound. We were laughing and having fun, so I said to her, "Mommy, do that down here," pointing to my private part. She told me, "We don't do that." I insisted, "Yeah, put your mouth down here."

She then started asking me questions and was horrified by what she discovered. This is how my mom remembers finding out that her 3-year-old baby girl was being molested by the very people she trusted to care for me.

She immediately called the police and child protective services to make a report and start an investigation. She was told to never speak to that family again because the investigation was going to get messy. I started seeing a children's therapist. Her office was in an older Victorian-style building. I remember staring at the vintage white walls in the waiting area, feeling uncomfortable and just wanting to get it over with. The therapist had red, frizzy, curly hair and was soft and round in stature. I loved playing with the sand box she had in her office. She had a bookshelf of little people, buildings, trees, and cars. Sometimes I got to add water to my sand world creations. I was more concerned with playing than talking.

I do remember her attempting a type of hypnosis: I was to relax and envision a safe, happy place. I still remember a vision from one of those sessions of a park waterfall that was very peaceful and everything was purple. Boy, do I wish that purple vision could have really kept me safe from harm, but it didn't. I was a difficult child due to the abuse I endured and the absence of a father.

I loved my mama. I would always scoop my arm through hers every time we walked anywhere. I remember always wanting to sleep with her. It was extremely hard when I had to transition to being a big girl and sleep in my own bed. Demons attacked me and sexually abused me when I slept by myself. I had a major fear of being left alone at night because that's when most of the sexual abuse previously occurred. I had to talk myself into going to sleep because almost every time I shut my eyes, horror met me again.

MY SAFETY MASK OF LIES

I had lots of friends as a kid, but at the same time, I felt very alone. From a very early age, I developed a delusional fantasy world. It was my defense mechanism. I just wanted to fit in to what I thought was normal. I wanted to forget how my life began, tangled in sexual perversion. I did a lot of "make-believe." Acting was one of my favorite things to do. I would put together dances and comedic plays whenever friends came over and would have the adults watch. There was something about making people laugh that made me feel good about myself. The toys and activities I liked usually involved acting and make-believe. I liked to make up characters because I could be anyone I wanted to.

Unfortunately, I took that to the extreme throughout my life and developed a serious lying problem. I was smiling on the outside and tormented on the inside. This made it very difficult for my mom or anyone to help me with the inward demons I fought. It was hard to decipher what was true and what was part of my dysfunctional mindset. My make-believe, delusions, and lies made me feel safe. If no one could find the real me inside, maybe they couldn't hurt me. I was always searching for something and someone to make sense of my life.

STRANGE THINGS HAPPENING

As a young girl, there was a series of strange things that happened spiritually. I would know things before they happened. For example, one time I threw a temper tantrum because I couldn't leave the house without being dressed head to toe like Dorothy from *The Wizard of Oz*. That day, we went to pick up my Grandma Ruth from the airport, and when she saw me, she freaked out. When we got home, she made my mom take pictures of me opening the present Grandma brought me. I unwrapped the gift and it was a doll, and guess what she was wearing. The exact same outfit I had on. The shoes, socks, dress, and even our hair was the same.

Another strange moment was when my mom and her boyfriend carried me asleep into the horse race track. I repeated a number a couple of times as I was sleeping in his arms. My mom suggested that he bet on the horse with the number I was mumbling. He looked up the horse and found that horse was always a loser, so he didn't bet on it. Guess which horse won. That's right, the underdog won that day. If he would have bet on that horse, he would have won a lot of money. He tried asking me for a number every time he went to the track after that, but I never knew the winning horse's number again.

I always knew there was something different about me. There were several other situations like the examples I mentioned. It sounds like it was a pretty cool thing to experience, but it wasn't. These strange happenings isolated me more from others, because when I tried talking to people about it, they never really understood. In fact, I often felt misunderstood. My family wasn't religious in any way. We never regularly went to church, a mosque, a temple, or anything religious. We attended Easter or Christmas services with a friend maybe five times, but that's it. Spiritually, things were confusing to me.

WITCHCRAFT

At about age 11, I started getting involved with witchcraft. I consistently read horoscopes and was really interested in anything supernatural. How did I know things before they happened? Maybe I was psychic! I would search at stores for anything to help me find information on WICCA. I considered myself to be a good witch. I even sewed myself a black robe to wear during séances. I would cast spells on people and often attempted to communicate with spirits. This opened a realm of darkness in my life that I wasn't ready for. The nightmares intensified. I had hallucinations and visions of demons trying to choke me while I slept. A recurring nighttime experience was demons coming to touch me and rape me. I was not ready or equipped for the evil that I welcomed into my life through WICCA and Tarot Cards.

I became so entangled with negativity that I became suicidal. Not only that, but I developed a deep demonic hatred for my mother. I hated myself and I hated her. For some reason, I blamed her for all of my pain, which was unrealistic. When she became aware of how serious this momentum of hatred was building inside, she took me to therapy again. When the therapist found out I wanted to kill myself and wished my mom dead, as well, she admitted me.

CALL ME CRAZY

At age twelve, I was institutionalized in a mental hospital psych ward for depression and being suicidal. I was clinically diagnosed with bipolar disorder, which caused several dysfunctional actions and decisions in my life. I remember hopelessly gazing out the window as the dramatics of another patient flailing down the hallway with nurses in pursuit brandishing needles transpired in my peripheral vision. I gazed around the room, numb and emotionless at the insane psych patients, realizing I was now one of them. I remember thinking about how crazy they were, as if my diagnosis of bipolar disorder, along with several other issues, made me any better than them.

After trial medications and medical professionals attempting to help me, in my mind, I concluded that there had to be something more. There had to be someone or something that could break me out of my inward cell of trauma, abuse, and torment. I didn't feel like my life was worth anything. I was searching, and nothing satisfied the huge void I had on the inside.

I quickly learned the system in the psychiatric hospital and how people were able to get out. So, I said everything I thought they wanted to hear and pretended to the best of my ability to play the role of someone "improving" from their condition. Once I was released, I begged my mom to take me off of the bipolar medications. I hated how it made me feel. This taught me that it was better to conceal my craziness. I knew if I talked about the demonic hallucinations or my depression, I would end up back in the hospital, so I kept it all to myself, internalizing more pain.

ABORTION ONE

I was 14 years old when I had my first boyfriend. I thought I was in love and couldn't get enough of being with him. He was a couple of years older than me and lived in the Buena Vista Apartments. Most of my friends lived in that several block radius known as "the BV's."

On my boyfriend's birthday, he took me to one of his friend's apartments across the street and told me that there was one gift that he wanted. He convinced me that I had to give him my virginity. We started drinking, which we usually did when we were together. I didn't even really know what to say, so I didn't say anything. I just did it. I laid there still and quiet. In my head were racing pictures and memories of sexual abuse from the past. I never knew how to tell someone "no" without the fear of something bad happening to me. I wanted to tell him I wasn't ready, that I didn't really like what we were doing, but he was my first boyfriend and I didn't want to disappoint him.

That was the beginning of being convinced almost every time we were together that we should have sex. One day, my mom approached me inquiring why I hadn't asked her to buy me any of my monthly toiletries. I didn't even realize that I had missed my period. I found out I was pregnant and it was decided that I was to get an abortion. So, at 14, I had my first abortion.

SMARTY PANTS

I always loved school. My high school achievements were one of the few things that I loved about myself. I really excelled in my classes and loved science. I took honors classes and even took a few college courses at the community college while in high school. I was nominated for and attended the National Youth Leadership Forum on Medicine at UCLA. I also had the privilege of going to a science class/program at Stanford for high school students interested in that field. I was able to hide behind good grades and academic honors. Here I was, a social butterfly, doing exceptionally well in school, yet completely broken and hurting on the inside.

ALCOHOL AND DRUGS

I didn't know how to feel better about myself. I didn't know how to recover from all of the trauma I had endured. So, I self-medicated. I would take vodka to school in water bottles and go to class drunk. No one ever knew because I hid it all so well. I started doing ecstasy and soon after, found someone who sold acid. The very thing that I thought would take away my pain and numb my tormenting thoughts and feelings only made things worse.

RAPED BY A STRANGER

I met a guy who was over 21 through some friends and saw him as a great opportunity to get free alcohol. I always kept my eyes open for someone to buy me alcohol. I was such a stupid, naïve girl... I thought I was using him for alcohol, and he ended up using me for so much more.

Something about that drink he got for me hit me much harder than expected. I knew my limits and I had my favorites.

Strawberry Scisco tasted like candy and I drank it often. But this time, I blacked out. That hadn't happened before. I was able to open my heavy eyelids a couple of times only to see him naked on top of me.

When I snapped out of it, my clothes were off and I knew what had taken place. I had been raped. I felt like I deserved it. This was my second time hanging out with him. I didn't know him. I was more concerned about getting alcohol than about my safety. I obviously never called him again for "free" Strawberry Scisco, because it wasn't really free.

BISEXUAL?

After being raped, I played with the idea that maybe girls would treat me better than guys. I was part of the girls' volleyball team at school and a few of us spent way too much time together. I didn't actually have a relationship with a girl, but I thought I was bisexual. We drank and did ecstasy together on weekends. It was an escape from reality and became the highlight of my life at the time. Drugs, best friends, partying all night long, and no boys. I was confused and searching for anything and anyone who could make me feel happy, even if it was only for a moment.

ABORTION TWO

At age 16, I was in a relationship on and off for about a year. I got pregnant and was so scared. I went to the clinic on my high school campus and was actually able to make an appointment for an abortion without parental consent. I hid everything from my family, as usual. The only thing I needed from my boyfriend was a ride home after the procedure. They told me that I would be too drugged up to drive myself. Of course, he was nowhere to be found, so I went alone.

I could tell the doctor was burnt out and had had a busy day. I was crying when he entered the room and he said in an irritated tone of voice, "You are going to have to stop crying. You made this decision. Put your legs up and let's get you in position. I have a lot of patients to see." I was shocked by his statement. It hurt my feelings even more, but I needed him. I needed him to erase my mistake. I was more scared of getting in trouble at the moment than the lifetime of depression and guilt from killing my baby.

This time, I didn't have the cushion of health insurance, so I was awake during the abortion. They didn't even have the decency to cover the trash or bloody instruments before sitting me up. I saw the chunks of flesh and blood in the trash can. Is that my baby? I took time to recover in the waiting room, then lied to the nurse and told her my ride was waiting for me downstairs. No one was waiting for me. My boyfriend was nowhere to be found. The next day, I found him hugged up with another girl and kissing after school. I sunk to an all new low.

SALVATION

One of my friends invited me to a youth church service on a Tuesday night. We went and I accepted Jesus into my heart as my Lord and personal Savior. This is what I was searching for all my life. I became almost addicted to being at church. Every time the doors were open, I wanted to be there. I had so much I needed healing and deliverance from. I quickly moved to the altar every time they had a time for prayer at the conclusion of service. My hurts, demons, traumas, and pain were cut off of my life one by one. This new faith and God's love were the only things that actually worked. Nothing else in life helped me. I found my help, my salvation.

There was one Friday night Holy Ghost service in particular that I will never forget. Collapsed across the altar in a heap with tears in my eyes and makeup and mascara running all over my face, the Lord called me into ministry. A majority of the masses of tired and hungry people had already left the church building, gotten into their cars, and driven off in search of any restaurant open late night on a Friday. I had just recently been saved. I still didn't really understand the whole Christianity thing. I attempted to sit myself up and pull my tangled, sweaty, hot hair away from my face and I heard God's voice again.

In the following weeks, people came up to me at different times speaking into my life, saying things like, "You have a purpose." "You've got a calling on your life." "God has an anointing on you for ministry." "God is going to send you to the Nations." What did all of that mean? Surely God had the wrong person! How could He use someone so messed up and broken? I already had more life experiences than most seasoned women in old age, and not the good kind. It was hard for me to believe that God would see anything valuable in me. I had a childhood of sexual abuse, had been raped, was suicidal, and struggled with drugs and alcohol, as well as dysfunctional relationships, and already had two abortions. There was no way I could be used for anything good!

Despite my feelings of unworthiness, I could not deny that He touched me that night and spoke to my heart. Little did I know, the path ahead of me would not be easy. Every time I stepped away from the Truth that set me free, I found myself bound again. I experienced salvation and a God calling, but I still didn't know how to deal with troubles, attacks, and hard times. I didn't yet have the tools and wisdom of how to fight for my purpose. Additionally, there were some legalistic teachings that I was consistently exposed to, which made me feel like I was so unworthy and unholy.

EX-BOYFRIEND MURDERED

About a year after my second abortion and break up with my ex-boyfriend, I got horrific news—he had been murdered!

Someone shot him in the head while he was sleeping in a car. He had a very troubled life. After we broke up, he moved away for a little bit and when he moved back to the area, something was different. He started stealing from several people and ended up in jail. I visited him a couple of times and actually picked him up from his grandma's house and took him to church with me. I connected with the broken boy on the inside and wanted him to experience the same freedom I had. I tried encouraging him and talking to him about God. I had no idea how dangerous his life had become and I couldn't believe that he had been murdered. This added another layer of guilt and shame from having my second abortion. I wondered, "Was I any different from the person who shot him?"

BEGINNING TO BE USED BY GOD

I drew closer and closer to God. I would spend hours in my prayer and Bible study time. I started getting a few opportunities to teach and preach. It was exciting to be used by the Lord. I became aware of gifts and talents within and better understood why there were always "strange things happening" in my life even from childhood and why I was different. Everything about me started making sense. I was attending San Francisco State University and enjoyed ministering to strangers to and from school, and everywhere I went. One of those strangers became a friend, then a boyfriend, and eventually asked me to marry him.

RAPED BY SOMEONE I LOVED

I was convinced that since we were getting married, it was okay to have sex. What a lie! I started feeling convicted and had a conversation with my fiancé that I had decided to wait until we were married to have sex again. He didn't really like that, but accepted my decision.

Soon after that conversation, I discovered that he had a porn addiction. I found VHS videos of porn all over his room. I confronted him about it. After that discovery, I started distancing myself from him.

One day, I came to his house to talk, and as we sat on his bed, something changed in him. He ripped off my clothes, held me down, and said, "Your body is mine. You belong to me. I can have you whenever I want you." He raped me. This was even worse than being raped by a stranger because I loved him. This was the person I thought I was going to marry. I was devastated and confused. I was trying to live for God. How could this happen to me? I was lost, angry, and extremely alone. The trauma caused me to blame God and run from Him instead of running to Him.

STRIPPER

Soon after that, my living situation changed. I felt like I had nowhere to go. I was desperate and had no money. So, I did what many girls in the state of California do when they feel rejected, hopeless, and homeless... I became a stripper. I found a strip club a long drive away from where I lived. It was a "no contact" all-nude strip club. Luckily, my step-sister's mom had an immediate opening in the apartment complex she owned. I told her I had no money, but I would get it to her quickly. I was able to move in with no deposit and no first month's rent. I was so thankful that I had a place to live. I made the money quickly and was able to pay all of my bills. I did discover, however, that quick money wasn't easy money.

One night as I was leaving work early in the morning, I got into my hunter green Ford Escort and discovered that something was wrong with one of my tires. The highway was only a few blocks from the club and my tire blew out as I was entering the onramp. I called A. A. A. Within a very short period of time, a tow truck arrived. It didn't say A. A. A., but I figured they must have dispatched it because it was the closest tow truck in the area.

I engaged in small talk with the driver. Then he opened the passenger side door to the tow truck and I got in. He was taking a very long time to hook up my car to his truck. I had free tow miles with A.A.A. and was just going to have my car towed home to deal with the tire in the morning.

I began wondering what was taking so long when a real A. A. A. Tow Truck arrived. The real A. A. A. guy got out of his truck and talked to the man whose truck I was in. Then the A. A. A. driver quickly came to me and yelled through the window, "Ma'am, this man is not a A. A. A.-contracted driver. I don't know who he is. Do you want to come with me?" I sensed that something wasn't right by the intensity in his voice. I looked down at the panel of the passenger side door to open the truck and get out. The door was completely gutted! There was no handle, no way to roll down the window, nothing. I was scared. I told the A. A. A. guy to open the door from the outside because I couldn't get out. He made the guy let me out of the truck.

Thank God that the A.A.A. man showed up when he did! Who knows what would have happened to me? I felt like it was a scene in a horror movie and I had just escaped a gruesome death.

ATTEMPTED SUICIDE

I was extremely depressed and drinking daily. I felt worthless. I met a guy who was visiting home on break from college. He was a friend of some of my friends, a good boy. He knew that I was a stripper and still wanted to be with me. His parents were in ministry and his family was very fun and loving. I think he wanted to save me from myself because he saw that underneath all of my pain and sin, there was someone good deep inside.

One night, I was fighting depression like never before. I was drinking and thinking about my life. I didn't want to live anymore. I made the decision to end my life. I grabbed one of my new butcher knives and began cutting. I wasn't doing this just for attention, but seriously trying to kill myself. There was blood running down my body and all over my apartment. I called my boyfriend to say "bye" to him. It was over. I gave up on myself.

But God didn't give up on me. In that moment, God showed me the same vision He showed me when He explained my calling to me years ago. I saw crowds and multitudes of people hurting, bound, and needing God. I was standing on an outside ministry platform, like a crusade in another country, looking into their lives and ministering freedom, truth, and love. Then I saw myself embracing hopeless, broken, diseased people and they were healed. The Lord gave me a glimpse of what I was born to do. He spoke to my heart as I was drunk, soaked in my own blood, and about to end it all. He said to me, "You can't die. Who will minister to the people I created you to reach?"

I saw another vision of all of the thousands of people in the previous vision lined up in front of me waiting. In that moment, God saved my life again. He didn't let me die. I felt His unexplainable love. He showed me that my life was valuable, I had a purpose, and He needed me. This was the conclusion of a six-month career as a stripper. Almost losing my life was a major shift in my path and journey. My boyfriend wanted me to move with him to Missouri and go to college with him. It was a fresh start, a new life. So I moved from the state of California to the state of Missouri with my boyfriend. Once I got there, I got a job as a phlebotomist in a hospital and enrolled for school full-time. Life was good again; at least for a little while.

ABORTION THREE

We should not have moved in together, but I enjoyed playing the "wife role," cooking, cleaning, and doing laundry. We went to church together, read our Bibles together. We really tried to keep purity in our relationship. I understood why people at church always said that you shouldn't live together until marriage. We had sex like one and a half times—meaning one of those times, we started and felt convicted, then stopped. I told myself it didn't count since we stopped. Silly me, silly me!

Well, the conclusion was that I got pregnant. He told me that I had to get an abortion, that I couldn't do this to him and that his parents could never find out. He was supposed to be a professional baseball player and there were scouts checking him out at college. He told me that if I had that baby, it would ruin his life. I felt so much pressure and knew that he was forcing me to get an abortion, so I did.

This time was different than the previous two. I felt that I was old enough to try and raise that baby, even if it was going to be hard. I just didn't want my baby growing up without a father like I did. I didn't feel like I had any other option than to just do what he said. He told me that having the baby would ruin his life, but killing the baby ruined mine.

POST-TRAUMATIC STRESS DISORDER

After the abortion, I found myself in that very familiar place of depression. I had a series of panic attacks and anxiety attacks. The night we came home from the abortion, I cried and screamed for hours. Staring at the wall, I rocked back and forth and screamed, "I want my baby!" Almost immediately after the abortion, my boyfriend went back to the state of California on break. I stayed faithful, paid the bills, kept the apartment clean, and tried to heal from my pain. I started seeing a counselor who diagnosed me with Post-Traumatic Stress Disorder (PTSD).

While my boyfriend was away, our relationship changed. He didn't text or call as much and I knew something was up. I found out he was talking to other girls, so I ended the relationship. I moved into my own apartment and made sure his apartment and car were clean with all bills paid, leaving everything in order for him. I wanted to leave on a good note.

A handsome guy at the gym approached me the same week and asked me if I wanted to hang out sometime. How convenient, I could use him to get over my last relationship. I started talking to him. I had previously resisted his attention at the gym—all of his subtle flirty gestures and smiles—since I wanted to be faithful while I was in a relationship. We started dating and before I knew it, I had jumped into another relationship. I guess focusing on someone else helped me not deal with the hurt I felt from the guy who forced me to get an abortion. This new catch wasn't as beautiful on the inside as he was on the outside. I didn't know that he had drug problems, lying problems, and was mentally "off." I didn't find all of that out until I let him move in with me. He was easy on the eyes and took my mind off of the PTSD I was dealing with. Anything to escape my messed-up reality, right?

The only good thing that came out of this new relationship was that he took me with him one time to Solid Rock Family Church in Jefferson City, Missouri. I was home. This was the church I was searching for the whole time I was in Missouri. This was just what I needed to help me through the anxiety and depression. The presence of God was in that building and the Word the pastor preached always seemed to be about the exact thing that I was dealing with.

POVERTY

When I found Solid Rock Family Church, I broke up with the latest boyfriend, moved out, and started really digging deep into God. I let him stay in my old apartment, because I didn't want there to be a reason for him to come back into my space. I took only the bare minimum with me. God was all that I had. I worked part-time at the laboratory and went to school full-time. I only had money to pay my rent and bills with very little left for food. I had no furniture in my new apartment. I slept on the floor with my big comforter, a pillow, and a lamp. That was all I had, aside from a few boxes of books, personal belongings, and a suitcase of clothes.

I walked four miles to school and four miles home. I could only afford to buy oatmeal, ramen noodle soup, and eggs. I remember crying when I went to the store because I was so hungry. There were a few times that I was so embarrassed for others to see my daily container of oatmeal that I ate lunch in the bathroom stall at school. It was hard for me to watch people buying hot dogs, pizza, and sodas. I started dropping a lot of weight and was skinnier than I had ever been. I had too much pride to ask the church to help me and didn't even realize that they would.

MEETING JOHN MARK SKILES

At Solid Rock, I ran every week to the place that I knew wouldn't fail me... the altar. Every time an invitation was made to come forward for prayer, I was there. In fact, that was the first place that John ever really noticed me. He saw me crying and broken on the altar, and through all of my pain, he saw my heart and knew there was something good on the inside. Pastor John was the Worship Leader and the Single's Pastor at the time. He approached me to connect with the singles and college student ministry and we exchanged numbers. When I first met him, I immediately felt a connection and attraction to him. However, I felt so messed up inside that I stopped myself from developing any kind of feelings for him. There was no way that a pastor would ever be interested in me!

We talked on the phone often and started building a really great friendship. Since we laughed a lot together, it was like we had always been friends. One time, we went on a "friend date." We went to see the movie *Santa Clause 2: The Mrs. Clause* and it was horrible, so we left. We drove to his mom and dad's house to hang out for a while. I thought it was so cool that I got to go over to my pastor's house. John's mom decided that she wanted to take a picture of us. Then he took me to his house to show me where he lived and introduced me to his roommate. I remember thinking, wow, I just got a tour of his life all in one night. We had such a fun time hanging out.

Very soon after that, I got scouted out for modeling in Los Angeles by a connection of someone I met last time I was home visiting in California. I told my new BFF John that I was moving back to California. He was disappointed that I was moving. I asked him to take me to the airport shuttle and he did. On the way, he told me that he would have loved to continue getting to know me and possibly date me, if I was staying. I couldn't believe that he actually had some kind of interest in me. Part of me wished that he would have told me sooner. Maybe that would have changed how lonely I was in Jefferson City. I had no idea that the pastor who I was saying goodbye to would later become my husband.

MODEL/ACTRESS

I was 20 years old and overwhelmed with excitement about being signed to a modeling management company in Los Angeles. I had just moved to L.A. and had immediately started auditioning and doing some small-time modeling and acting work. Modeling wasn't as easy and fun as I thought it would be. I got about one out of every ten auditions that I went to.

Auditioning took a lot of time, energy, and sitting in L.A. traffic. I developed an eating disorder during my modeling days. I wasn't skinny enough or tall enough, and had too many curves to get into the magazines and runway shows that I dreamt about, so I ended up in urban men's magazines. Definitely not my dream come true, but I thought maybe that was just the beginning.

I became bulimic and would actually have a panic attack if I was not able to throw up my food quickly enough. I hid this problem from everyone. How surprising... wearing my "safety mask of lies" became my comfort zone yet again. I ended up doing a couple of small roles in movies and found the most pleasure in acting.

Acting was an escape from the reality of my painful life, especially during my childhood. I found comfort in it again. I would practice monologues in my room, work on creating characters, and study all of the books and info I could find. I wasn't spectacular on camera, to be honest, but I was a "work in progress." I thought that if I made it in acting, I would use that platform to help people.

I went to auditions during the day and partied all night. Me and my girls loved the VIP treatment. We refused to stand in lines and enjoyed partying in luxury. I actually got paid to be a model hostess at parties and events. We would dance, drink, and laugh all night. We were the pretty comedian girls that were always the life of the party and made everywhere we went a "fun place." In the midst of this, it was really hard to find real friends. Me and my sister/BFF always found ourselves around celebrities and, honestly, didn't see them as anything more than talented people who had excelled in their crafts.

We thought asking for autographs and pictures with celebs was just trashy. We would constantly have to weed out friends once we discovered they were groupies and couldn't handle the lifestyle. We never knew who were real friends until time told the truth about them and we had to cut them off. So, we had a lot of fun, but lots of drama, too; there were some crazy situations. There were also some insane stalkers, which came with the territory of being a men's magazine model and a professional drunken partier. When alcohol is part of the daily routine, I guess drama and craziness are inevitable.

SEX TRAFFICKING

One day, I got a call that I was hired for a modeling job in another country. I was told that I would be a model and hostess at an event for a billionaire's clothing line. I had heard of event hostess jobs like that before, so it didn't seem odd to me. In fact, I was extremely excited! I would get to stay at his famous resort and get paid to be a model at an event for his clothing line. I looked up this resort online and big-name celebrities had been there. This was the place that millionaires went for vacation. His clothing line was well known and sold in stores, so everything checked out.

I shared my excitement with my family, that I had an opportunity to spend Christmas in another country! I talked it up so much to my mom and a couple of other family members and friends, because this was "the best modeling job ever!" I was told to be ready for the event upon arrival. I had a one-way ticket, which should have been a red flag.

As soon as I got off of the plane, I changed and touched up my makeup in a bathroom. This was it! I was a world-traveling MODEL! A man in a Hummer picked me up and took me to the resort. When we drove onto the property, I was in disbelief of how beautiful this place was. He took me up to a bedroom and put down my suitcase, telling me this is where I would be staying. He left quickly as I began asking him, "Is this someone else's room?" I saw personal belongings there and it seemed like this room was being lived in. Maybe I was rooming with one of the other models.

Almost instantly, the billionaire came in and I figured out that I was actually in his master bedroom. He greeted me by grabbing my boobs, telling me how sexy I was, and how much fun we were going to have. This shocked me, but I had dealt with perverts before in the entertainment industry. So much was running through my mind. Why did that guy take me to his master bedroom? It must have been a mistake.

I met another girl as we were on our way to this event that I was hired for. She was sweet, but really didn't look like a model to me. When we arrived at the event, there was no red carpet, no marketing material for his clothing line, and no professionals managing or organizing anything. It was just a club. We were escorted in by security to a VIP table. I was so confused and scared. I was trying to put all of the pieces together in my head. I started drinking, something that was already very much a part of my life. I needed a drink, because this whole situation didn't feel right and seemed crazy to me.

The girl I met earlier pulled me in close while the billionaire was socializing. She warned me saying, "Just do whatever he says. Be good. I don't want the same thing to happen to you that happened to the girl they just sent away. She wouldn't have sex with him and he brutally raped her, beat her, and did some really crazy stuff to her sexually. Anal stuff. Just do whatever he says. He is really nice to girls that are 'good.' He says he's going to get my teeth fixed with veneers." Those were not exactly her quoted words, but that's what I remember her saying in that conversation. She also told me to watch what I say on the phones at the resort, "because they listen."

We drove back to the resort after the party was over. I had so much fear inside and didn't know what to do. Here I was, a 20-year-old stupid, stupid girl tricked into flying to another country with a one-way ticket for a "modeling job" and no money to go home. My cell phone didn't work, because I never switched it to an international plan. I couldn't say anything on the phone lines because "they listen." No one had the phone number to the resort to contact me. I felt trapped.

How did this happen? What was he going to do to me? If I was good, he would be nice to me. If I was bad, I would be brutally raped and beaten. I had been raped twice before in my life; I knew what that felt like. So, I opted for option A, "Be good." That night, out of fear, I slept with a monster. The next morning, I went down for breakfast and got a tour of the resort. I had so many conflicting feelings inside. It was the most beautiful place I had ever seen. White sands, clear water, it looked like paradise.

However, paradise was paired with one of the most despicable sexual encounters I'd ever experienced. It was one more ugly episode to add to the collection of the perverse violations my body endured in life. So, here I was, thinking about horrible things while walking through paradise. I got a massage almost every day. I always kept an alcoholic beverage in my hand, doing anything to keep my mind off of the fact that at any moment he could call me back to the dungeon of his room. I had to stay numb. I couldn't process or understand what had happened to me and how I was going to get home. I told myself over and over, "Just survive, Sula, just survive."

I called my mom and a few others from my room phone line. In my mind, I tried to think about how I could tell them and maybe get a ticket home, but I couldn't say anything on the phone lines; plus, I was so ashamed for getting into this mess. It was easier for me to pretend like nothing happened. I just told them about how beautiful it was there and I wasn't sure when I would be coming home. I don't know why, but I lied. I convinced them that I was spending "Christmas in Paradise."

Every night, more girls showed up for dinner, which was the routine. We all had to dress up and be there promptly on time. Some of the girls were from that country and some from other places. After dinner, he would select the girl of his choice and they had to sleep with him. One night, he called on three of us to come up to his room. The next day, the two girls he selected with me got tickets to fly home. So, I asked the billionaire if I could leave and have a plane ticket, as well. He said, "No," and that I needed to stay because he had someone that I was supposed to meet... his girlfriend. He told me that he purchased me as a

Christmas gift for her... WHAT?

So, the pieces of this sick, twisted story came together. I was a young girl purchased as a Christmas gift, lied to, and tricked into coming to another country with the expectation of a modeling job. At that time, I didn't know what sex trafficking was, I didn't know there was actually a name for the evil I was experiencing. I saw many more horrific things during those three weeks held captive, things that were too graphic and painful to even talk about, things that no one should ever have to go through.

I was finally able to convince the girlfriend to get me a ticket home and allow me to leave by telling her that I would continue to be with her. It's crazy how "Stockholm Syndrome & Complex Trauma" work. I told her I just needed to go home and take care of a few things. When I got home, I changed my contact info. Shortly after, I even saw the girlfriend out in the crowd a couple of times at L.A. parties. I was kind to her, but acted like nothing ever happened. I'm not sure if I consciously or subconsciously did this, but the sex trafficking was literally erased from my memory and the trauma was fractured and suppressed until years later. I lived for years as if I was never trafficked, completely unaware that it happened to me.

RELATIONSHIP FLOPS

After the sex trafficking experience, I returned to the Hollywood party scene. I acted like everything was great and literally erased the previous events from my thoughts. I continued small-time modeling and acting, but I wasn't making enough money to support myself. I got a job as a licensed phlebotomist, drawing blood and doing lab work. I always fell back on the medical field, because it was easy for me to find work since I was nationally certified to do that kind of work.

I ended up in a couple of relationships as I continued "looking for love in all the wrong places." One of those relationships was full of passion, intensity, and drunken, abusive fights. He was one that I thought I would always be with. Together, we were toxic, a combustive combination. He wasn't faithful to me, but when he was with me, he loved me so much that I overlooked all of the other issues. After a bloody swollen lip and a fight, there was no turning back from finally sealed the deal on that one.

The next relationship flop was with a prince. I dated him for about a year. I also lived with him and traveled all over the world to Brazil, Paris, Switzerland, Hawaii, and Mexico. He was the most charming man I have ever met. He had a great sense of humor and kept me laughing. I thought I was the only woman in his life and we were hardly ever separated. He spoiled me and took care of me. Unfortunately, behind all of that charm, his huge smile, and frequent words, "I love you," there were many things that I wasn't aware off... including other women. I had to get out of that relationship because, although living like a princess is every little girl's dream, it wasn't a healthy relationship. I made the decision that I would rather be broke, living in a cardboard box alone, than on top of the world with royalty while being cheated on and lied to.

A GOD CAVE

I retreated into what I call a "God Cave." I realized that after living with $30,000 shopping sprees, Gucci, Dolce & Gabbana, butlers, maids, chefs, assistants, security, Bentleys, Maseratis, private planes, and all of the things people dream of, that I wasn't fulfilling my life's purpose. I wasn't doing what I was born to do. I wasn't happy.

I started on a healing and deliverance journey yet again. I spent all day long in my Word, praying, and time in praise and worship. It seemed as though everything that I ever studied or learned of God in my life came back to me. I promised the Lord that I would never run from Him again. I didn't care where His purpose would take me, I would never resist His will again. That was the first time that I made that type of serious commitment to God. I had lived for Him before, preached and taught for Him before. I had prophesied and fasted and praised and worshiped for God before. But never with the determination and dedication of the commitment and decision I just made. I had seen poverty and I had seen royalty. After everything I went through, God became my everything again and the only One worth living for. I said "YES" to the calling on my life. I was done trying to live life for myself. I rededicated my life to Christ in total surrender.

MARRYING INTO MINISTRY

The Lord kept putting my old friend, Pastor John Mark Skiles, in my thoughts, so I would pray for him often. Finally, there was a week where I thought about him several times a day, and I knew that I needed to reconnect with him for some reason, but had no idea why. I looked up the church online and called Solid Rock in Jefferson City, Missouri. I left a message on his office phone. He called me back the next day. We were both so excited to reconnect and he said to me, "Sula! You're never going to guess what I found around the same time you called me yesterday... the picture my mom took of us four years ago! It was covered in dust under my bed. I never even knew it was there. Isn't that crazy?" I was shocked and said to God, "Wow, Lord, what are you doin'?" We talked forever and it was like we never missed a day.

Many conversations followed that initial call. We both began recognizing that God was up to something. During one of the calls, John shared his life story with me, including details that he never told any other girl before. He had been raped repeatedly as a little boy by a male family friend and, as a result, had many private struggles and confusion in life. However, God had healed him from that pain. I think he thought that after bearing all to me, maybe I would think of him differently. Something about knowing his story made me love him more. I said to him, "That's nothing, let me tell you my story!" So I did. We shared every dark secret with each other and there was no judgment, condemnation, or negativity.

One day, I was in prayer and felt the Lord overwhelmingly speak to me. He told me that John was the one I was to marry and spend my life with. WOW! I told the Lord that He would have to confirm that to John and that he would have to be the one to say it. I was not going to do what many had done to me before: "The Lord said that I am supposed to marry you!" Ha— they couldn't have been more wrong! I'm so glad I never followed through with empty proposals made to me in the past. This time, God revealed it to me personally so that I wouldn't have to guess. That night, John called me and said, "Don't freak out, but I'm going to marry you one day." I replied by saying, "I know." We both wanted more confirmation and many confirmations did come. God didn't waste any time.

The next day, John went to the public library. A stranger (Hebrews 13:2) approached him and said, "Are you a Christian leader of some sort?" He replied by saying, "Yes." She proceeded to tell him that God sent her there that day to give him a word. She said, "God has showed you the woman you are to marry. Yes, it is her. Don't worry about anything. He will bring her to you. Move forward in faith." The hair on the back of John's neck stood up and he knew that this was yet another undeniable confirmation that really sealed the deal. She disappeared after releasing the word to him. John searched the library for her to thank her. To this day, we're not sure if she was an angel.

Soon after the library event, I flew out to Missouri to visit him for a week and met the rest of his family. I enjoyed attending Solid Rock Family Church again and reconnecting with people. It was so cool to meet the pastoral staff that I would eventually be a part of.

Another interesting moment leading up to our marriage took

place on an evening when I was sitting on the couch at my family's house in California. I envisioned having a very simple and intimate backyard wedding with plush greenery and a beautiful elegant set up. Previously, we had only talked about getting married on the beach in Hawaii or someplace like that, but we knew it would be very expensive for family and friends to fly out and attend. Within a few moments of my daydreaming of the simple intimate family wedding, John called me. I could tell he had been crying. And I knew he was speaking from a God-moment he was experiencing. He said, "Don't freak out, but the Lord told me we are not supposed to wait or prolong this wedding. He showed me the date May 25th and I think we are supposed to keep it simple, maybe in my parents' backyard." I knew every word he was saying was the plan we were to follow. He then asked me to marry him officially over the phone. We already knew that was God's plan, but he realized he never officially asked. Of course, I said, "Yes," with tears in my eyes.

We got married about four months after our first reconnection conversation. We have been happily married ever since. Everything about life became brand new and my trauma cycle ended. I'm not saying that everything has been perfect, but I now had a new perspective of how to deal with attacks and adversities. We had each other to live out God's calling and fight for our purposes together.

HAPPILY EVER AFTER

God has healed me, delivered me, and set me free from the trauma, hurt, and pain of my life. Just the fact that I'm alive, completely physically healthy, sane, and happy today is proof that there is a God! There is no human way possible that I could have survived everything in my life all by myself without any help from someone up above. I have no more bipolar disorder, no more PTSD, no more depression, anxiety, or any form of mental illness. I'm excited to wake up every day and live a purpose-filled life. I'm at peace with my past and have forgiven those who've hurt me. I also have healthy relationships with my family. My husband and I love doing full-time ministry together.

One of God's greatest acts of redemption is in the births of our daughter and son who have great purpose on their lives. As church planters, we started a brand-new church in 2014, called "Impact Life Church," in the state of Florida (www.impactlifechurch.us). I also work locally and globally in the rescue and aftercare of trafficking victims as a Survivor Leader & Advocate. Today, I am a speaker, author, minister, and sex trafficking abolitionist! Who would have thought that anything great could ever come out of my life? I enjoy sharing my story to help inspire others, leading them into an intimate love relationship with Jesus. I am proof that a life of pain, sin, and trauma can be transformed into something inspirational.

I'm not saying all of this to brag or be prideful, but to encourage you. No matter what you have been through in life, God has a very special plan for you and you can absolutely be free from everything that has ever kept you bound. If God did it for me, He can't wait to do it for you! So now you're thinking, "Wow, that is an amazing story. How in the world did you get to where you are today?" Let me tell you.

PART TWO_

2.1 THE BASICS_

Two of the most common philosophical, scientific, and religious questions asked among human beings are "What's my purpose?" and "Why am I here?" In life's journey, we begin wondering if there is something more to our existence than what we are experiencing.

In Part Two of this book, I pray that you discover what took me many years to find. If you grab hold of the truth and tools presented here, I believe that your life will be transformed. God uniquely created you to fulfill a purpose. There is no one else like you. You were wonderfully and fearfully made in the image of God (Psalm 139:14). I like to imagine God looking down at the world, scratching His head and thinking to Himself, "Hmm... something is missing." Then, realizing what the world needed, He created you!

There are people that only you can impact that others may never cross paths with. Everything about you can be used for God's glory. Your personality, talents, where you were born, the family that raised you, what you look like, your circle of friends, the schools you attend, places you've worked... even a testimony of trauma and pain can be transformed into a life of power and victory. I have seen that to be very true. Everything that composes your life and where you are today can conclude in the fulfillment of a divine purpose.

We are not to just walk through life aimlessly. You were not created to just live a mediocre life of complacency. Do you feel like your life is bland, normal, "just average," "nothing special," boring, and you're just "going through the motions?" If so, it should not be that way; God has so much more for you! When you find your purpose in life and begin to live it, nothing can describe the joy, adventure, awe, wonder, satisfaction, and fulfillment that you will experience.

How do we even begin to answer the age-old question, "What's my purpose?" The easiest way to analyze the answer to this question is first to look at "the big picture." We must first have an understanding of why we were created before we can define our specified function in life.

GOD'S LOVE

God is absolutely in love with you. In fact, 1 John 4:8 says, "God is love." I believe that He Himself, being love and having so much love, wanted that love reciprocated back to Him. He yearned for family. Being love, He wanted someone to love Him. He therefore created mankind to be in fellowship with Him, to experience a love relationship with Him. He created us for His glory (Isaiah 43:7).

God could have created us to automatically love Him, but then there would always be the question, "Do they really love Me?" Real love involves a choice to love when other options exist. When you marry someone, do you want them to marry you because you forced them to do it or because they chose of their own free will to love you and commit to you? This is why we have a choice.

The very fact that the enemy and evil is even allowed to exist creates a choice. God is a gentleman and won't force us to do anything against our own will. The problem with the existence of evil is that it creates temptation and the issue of sin. Man, being imperfect, released our authority over sin in the garden, but through Jesus' death on the cross, we gained it back (1 Corinthians 15). God gave us a resolution to this sin problem through sending us a Savior. John 3:16 says, "For God loved the world so much that he gave his one and only Son, so that everyone who believes in him will not perish but have eternal life."

God's love is nothing like man's. He will not violate, abuse, manipulate, sexually assault, abandon, talk down to, betray, cheat on, or trick you. He is not cruel, nor does He operate in confusing toxic aggression. He is good and pure and His love is unfailing. He is faithful, kind, honest, and true. If you have a warped understanding of God's love—meaning that it's really hard for you to receive love or feel worthy of love—it's probably because people have been twisted in the way that they showed "love" to you. We will talk more about healing emotional pain in later chapters. For now, please believe that you are lovable and God desires to continually live close to you. He wants to awaken your ability to experience the many facets of His love.

By God's grace through Jesus, we are able to be forgiven, freed from sin, and enter into an intimate love fellowship with Him. Through Jesus, we are seated with Him in a position of authority over evil (Ephesians 2:6). We are reconnected to the One who is in love with us. When you are separated from the one you love, you can become heartbroken or lovesick. Our sin once separated us from God. I can't even imagine how much that must have grieved Him, but I'm so glad that we were reconciled to God through the death of His Son (Romans 5:10). As we choose to live for Him, our dedicated love means something, because we sacrifice all else and refuse to entertain other options and temptations. Our heart belongs to Him alone! We become a part of a royal family!

IN THE END

The One who is love is looking for a Bride for His Son (Matthew 22:2-14). In the end of it all, God's desire is that we spend eternity in heaven with Him. The conclusion of the Bible describes our entry into heaven as a wedding celebration (Revelation 19:7-10, 22:17). The relationship between Jesus and His people is depicted as a bride and bridegroom in both the Old and New Testaments. We are to be faithful and committed to Him as we are betrothed to one Husband (2 Corinthians 11:2). The affection of Jesus toward us brings satisfaction to our soul like nothing and no one else ever could. In the end, He will come into a covenant marriage relationship with those who chose to believe in Him and truly love Him. He who is love will experience His love reciprocated for eternity. This is God's desire and therefore becomes the heart and soul of our purpose. I invite you to read my book *His Beloved Bride: A Journey into Deeper Intimacy with Jesus* to learn how to live from the reality of this powerful revelation.

When you find the love of Father God through faith, it is so amazing that you want everyone you know to experience it. You are so special to God. Titus 2:14 says that He purifies for Himself His own special people. It becomes our job to help others understand how special they are to God, as well. We are commissioned to share God's love through spreading the Good News.

Your life is one piece in a gigantic puzzle. The final result is an eternal love relationship with God. Our general purpose is to share God's love and truth through witnessing to the world around us. You are able to do that in whatever job or dream that you may have. There are ways to be the light of the world in everything that you do (Matthew 5:14).

God's plan for your life is even more specific than who you generally are as a Christian. He uniquely created you to fulfill a specific purpose on earth. Before you were even formed in your mother's womb, God knew you (Jeremiah 1: 4-8). It is so important that you trust God with your life. Please believe that His plan for you is so much better than anything you could put together! He is Almighty God, the Creator of the universe, the Beginning and the End, the Alpha and Omega. Don't you think He is trustworthy? The same hands that shaped and molded you into existence are also holding your future. "My future is in your [God's] hands" (Psalm 31:15). You may not have all of the details of each aspect of God's plan for you, but trust me, it's going to be good! God isn't just "winging it" and He knows what He's doing. Ephesians 2:10 says, "For we are God's masterpiece. He has created us anew in Christ Jesus, so we can do the good things he planned for us long ago." You have to believe that your life is valuable and special and know that there is a reason why you are alive today.

EVERY CHRISTIAN'S LIFE ASSIGNMENT

Second Peter 3:9 explains that God "does not want anyone to be destroyed, but wants everyone to repent." In trying to find our purpose and destiny in life, it is imperative that we understand the agenda and master plan of God. We have to get serious and be about our Father's business (Luke 2:49). We are to be His agents on earth representing Him. We are not to be on a search to fulfill "our will" on this earth, but to understand what God's desires are and then carry them out through our lives. As much as we would like to think life is all about us... it's not!

A mission without the Great Commission is not a God Mission. The harvest of souls is directly connected to your life's purpose. It is your life assignment. The Great Commission is explained in Matthew 28:19-20. Paraphrased, it says that all Christians are commissioned by the Lord Jesus to spread the Gospel and make disciples, while baptizing them and teaching them the ways of the Lord. That is God's purpose for all of us. Each of us were created to be able to accomplish that task in different ways.

Don't box in titles and roles, thinking that because you're not called to be a pastor, you don't have to share the Gospel with anyone. In fact, our love relationship with God should develop compassion in us for others. We become the "Good Samaritan" who doesn't just pass by broken and hurting people (Luke 10:25-37). Evangelism is an everyday lifestyle, not just a task out of obligation or religious duty. You can fulfill God's purpose for your life with your family, on your job, and with everyone you interact with. Let your passion for the Lord compel you.

There is so much joy from the Lord when you impact someone's life through Him. If you have been stagnant in your faith, I encourage you to step out and pray for someone who is sick; share Jesus and watch Him do a miracle. Self-focused Christians are not happy. Sometimes Christians get stuck in religious patterns of just going to church on Sunday with zero excitement, passion, and joy. That's usually because they have compartmentalized God to one hour on a Sunday and there is no fulfillment in their soul because faith and purpose have not become a lifestyle yet. It's time to go all in!

Jesus said in John 17:17-18, "Make them holy by your truth; teach them your word, which is truth. Just as you sent me into the world, I am sending them into the world." If we are called and sent into the world just as God sent Jesus, then we must understand what Jesus was sent into the world to do. This is vital information for us as we seek to discover what we're supposed to be doing with our lives. Knowing what Jesus was sent into the world to do will answer part of that question, "What's My Purpose?"

Luke 19:10 says, "For the Son of Man came to seek and save those who are lost." You will discover your purpose as you find an avenue to fulfill the Great Commission, finding ways to seek and save those who are lost. There are people that you talk to daily that need to hear Jesus was born of a virgin, died on the cross for their sins, was buried, and on the third day rose from the dead with all power in His hands. He is now sitting on the right hand of the Father interceding for them, and through confessing and believing that Jesus is Lord, they are saved. Your co-workers, friends, and family members need to know that there is a God who loves them and holds the answer to all of their problems. They need to know that healing miracles and freedom from mental and emotional pain is possible through Christ. I've seen, with my own eyes, Jesus perform countless healing miracles and deliverance in the lives of people He brings across my path. The Gospel is TRUTH and it's what the world needs!

Your life is like an open book to those around you. They read your words and actions, whether you like it or not. The way you live your life is a witness of who God is. People will analyze your life and will either want what you have or would rather do without it. How well do you represent God? If you can't offer broken people more than they already have, then they will not be interested in your witness. This is why you have to find total freedom in your life! Not just for you, but for everyone around you that needs a Savior.

There should be something different about you, something that attracts people to God. Jesus says that we are the "salt of the earth" (Matthew 5:13). When you really comprehend what being the salt of the earth means, life becomes flavorful. There should be something magnetic about you that brings joy, love, peace, excitement, and encouragement to everyone you know. You should bring flavor to everyone you come in contact with. One of the characteristics of salt is that it makes you thirsty. You should be so excited about God that the people around you become thirsty for God and want to know more about Him. People's lives should be changed when you are around. As Jesus is, so are we in the world (1 John 4:17). You have much more potential for your life than you realize. It is imperative that you get free enough and empowered enough to live up to God's full potential for you. Dig deep and rediscover who you are and what you can accomplish. Don't let anything or anyone stop you from accomplishing something great in your lifetime.

John 14:12 says, "I tell you the truth, anyone who believes in me will do the same works I have done, and even greater works, because I am going to be with the Father."

KNOW WHO YOU ARE

Now you have an understanding of the reason for your creation and every Christian's life assignment. When trying to understand the basics, you must also understand your personal identity. There are many Scriptures that define the very nature of what God has made every Christian to be. It is God's desire and plan for you to know who you are. You have to get rid of the old way you have viewed yourself and align your beliefs about yourself with God's perspective of who you are. In order to discover God's personal agenda for your life, you must know who you really are. You can't live out God's plan with old feelings and mindsets about yourself.

SELF-WORK

Take a moment and describe yourself below. Who are you? Include the good, the bad, and the ugly. What do you think and believe about yourself? Be honest, or this simple exercise won't work.

_____
_____
_____
_____
_____

Now, read the following Scriptures. This is how God describes you. It may be hard to see all of His beautiful truths about you right now because maybe they haven't been understood or believed enough yet. Please read these out loud; they are written in affirmation form so that you can apply the Word personally through proclamation. Read them, speak them, and pray them until you fully believe them and God's perspective of you becomes your perspective of yourself.

- Corinthians 5:17—I am a new person. My past is forgiven and everything is new.
- Matthew 5:14—In Jesus, I am the light of the world.
- John 1:12—I am a child of God.
- John 15:15—I am Christ's friend.
- Psalm 139:14—I am fearfully and wonderfully made.
- Romans 8:17—I am a co-heir with Christ, inheriting His glory.
- 1 Corinthians 3:16, 6:19—I am a temple, a dwelling place for God.
- 1 Corinthians 6:17—I am joined forever to the Lord and I am one spirit with Him.
- Ephesians 1:1; Philippians 1:1; Colossians 1:2—I am a saint, a Holy person.
- Ephesians 2:10—I am God's building project, His handiwork, created to do His work.
- Colossians 3:12; 1 Thessalonians 1:4—I am chosen of God, holy and dearly loved.
- 1 Thessalonians 5:5—I am a child of light and not darkness.
- Romans 6:1-6—The sinful person I used to be died with Christ, and sin no longer rules my life.
- Romans 8:1—I am free from the punishment (condemnation) my sin deserves.
- 1 Corinthians 2:16—I have been given the mind of Christ. He gives me His wisdom to make right choices.

- 2 Corinthians 5:21—I have been made acceptable to God (righteous).
- Ephesians 1:3—I have been blessed with every spiritual blessing.
- 2 Peter 1:3—I have been given all things that pertain to life and godliness through my knowledge of Him (God), the One who has called me to glory and virtue.
- John 3:16—I am loved and eternally accepted!
- Ephesians 3:12—I may approach God with boldness, freedom, and confidence.
- Colossians 1:13—I have been rescued from the dark power of Satan's rule and have been brought into the kingdom of Christ.
- Colossians 1:14—I have been forgiven of all of my sins and set free. The debt against me has been cancelled.
- 2 Timothy 1:7—I have been given a spirit of power, love, and a sound mind.
- Colossians 2:11—I am spiritually clean. My old self has been removed.
- 1 John 5:18—I am born again in Christ, and the evil one, the devil, cannot touch me.
- Isaiah 54:17—No weapon formed against me shall prosper.
- Philippians 4:13—I can do all things through Christ who strengthens me.
- 1 Corinthians 15:57—I have the victory!
- Romans 8:37—I am more than a conqueror.
- 2 Corinthians 10:4—The weapons of my warfare are mighty through God.
- 1 John 4:4—Greater is He that's in me than he who is in the world.
- Psalm 27:1—The LORD is the strength of my life; of whom shall I be afraid?

- Hebrews 4:12—When I speak the Word, it is quick and powerful and sharper than a two-edged sword.
- Matthew 10:1; Mark 3:14-15; Mark 6:7; Luke 9:1—I am a disciple of Jesus, so I have authority over every unclean spirit and all sickness and diseases.

2.2 THE TRANSFORMATION_

> "This means that anyone who belongs to Christ has become a new person. The old life is gone; a new life has begun!" (2 Corinthians 5:17)

God makes all things new. In my opinion, one of the greatest things about our journey with God is the transformation process. My life was so broken and messed up and without God, I would have remained in the gutter. He really has made me a new creation, a new person. He turned every sinful, hurting, traumatized part of me into something new, something valuable, something usable. God offers another chance at life to everyone who comes to Him through the redemptive work of Jesus on the cross. The moment salvation occurs, a transformation begins in us.

The old life we had becomes nothing in comparison to the blessings, promises, authority, power, and inheritance we have as children of God. His desire for you is that all things become completely new. Your life as a believer should be full of excitement and joy, not weighed down with constant issues from the past and continual cycles of sin and negativity. We are to be transformed more and more into the character and image of Jesus Christ. You can't live out your God-destiny without allowing Him to transform you; He wants you to be complete in Him (Colossians 2:10). He is the only one who can fill the voids in your life so that nothing is missing. He makes us whole and He is what we have been searching for all along.

Some people allow this transformation to happen instantly and some fight it, ultimately delaying the process. I chose the latter, and as a result, probably went through many things that I didn't have to go through. Partial surrender does not result in total freedom. In order to live the new life God has for you, it is imperative that you learn how to die to some areas of your old life. This part is really not fun, but it is very much needed. We can't live life as we have always lived and expect to see anything different. There are some mindsets, characteristics, mannerisms, and actions that must be done away with because they are toxic.

This is something only God can do, but we do have a responsibility to turn away from certain negative thoughts, words, and actions. "Submit yourselves, then, to God. Resist the devil, and he will flee from you" (James 4:7). When we submit and surrender everything to God, we are empowered to resist the enemy, and the devil literally has to run and leave us alone. But that type of power only comes through total surrender to God on our part. If you are having trouble resisting the enemy in a certain area, then ask God what part of you needs to fully surrender. We must freely receive the new life that God has promised us in Him by His immeasurable grace. Second Corinthians 7:1 says, "Because we have these promises, dear friends, let us cleanse ourselves from everything that can defile our body or spirit. And let us work toward complete holiness because we fear God."

This God-transformation is a daily process. Jesus said if anyone wants to come after Him, we must deny ourselves, "daily" pick up our cross, and follow Him (Luke 9:23). You can't just accomplish it once and then you never have to work at it again… it's a lifestyle change! The disciples gave up everything to follow Jesus (Luke 14:33). They left their jobs, communities, friends, family—everything! They understood the importance of letting go of the old to embrace what God had for them. You may not have to quit your job, sell everything you own, and start a street ministry for Jesus, but there should be nothing in life that comes before your relationship with Him and your ability to follow Him. This is not out of obligation, legalism, striving, or religious pressure, but out of your intimacy with the Lord that these things are possible.

This doesn't mean that you have to become a robot, lose your personality, or live a boring life. In fact, God created you to be unique, and your personality is part of who God made you to be. However, sometimes we pick up mindsets and mannerisms that are actually learned lies, behaviors from circumstances, or spiritual oppressions we've experienced, and we think they are part of who we are. Sometimes we struggle with letting go of certain perspectives and actions, defending them as being part of our personality. In actuality, our human nature builds defense mechanisms and seeks self-medication to try to fix ourselves. We build all of "who we are" based on what we've been through and all it takes is for the right storm in life to cause all of that to easily crumble.

God wants to rebuild our lives on the solid rock foundation of Jesus. Our fleshly human side can carry several pieces of baggage that we are unaware of until we completely surrender our lives to the Master's hands. I'm so glad that we are not responsible for fixing ourselves with our human strength.

God is the only one who can help you rediscover your true self. This life transformation can be full of awe and wonder as you have encounters with Him! You have to trust Him to make all things new. There are some things that you can pay attention to in order to embrace this process and eliminate delay. There are five major areas that require intentionality in your God-transformation.

1. THE FLESH

The flesh is your natural, human side composed of your will, emotions, attitude, mind, thoughts, desires, heart, etc. When you start living for God, you recognize that your natural, carnal, sinful nature is usually at war with His Word and His ways. "So I say, let the Holy Spirit guide your lives. Then you won't be doing what your sinful nature craves. The sinful nature wants to do evil, which is just the opposite of what the Spirit wants. And the Spirit gives us desires that are the opposite of what the sinful nature desires. These two forces are constantly fighting each other, so you are not free to carry out your good intentions" (Galatians 5:16-17).

If you're anything like me, whenever I went after my natural desires and my plan in life, things got messed up. The moment I realized that doing things my way didn't work and I submitted myself to God's way, everything in my life changed. Philippians 3:3 says, "We rely on what Christ Jesus has done for us. We put no confidence in human effort." We can't trust in ourselves more than we trust in God. Human effort accomplishes nothing (John 6:63). Don't assume you've got it all figured out, trusting in your own natural wisdom—that is the path to becoming a fool (Romans 1:22). You literally have to make a decision to cut out habits, relationships, hobbies, activities, and anything that you know causes you to get into a negative, unhealthy, and ungodly place. Indulging your natural fleshly desires (i.e., having those things or people in your life) is not worth the consequences. The Self-Work section at the conclusion of this chapter will help you determine what those things are. And once you recognize them, make a choice to NOT allow them to destroy your life any longer.

You have to stop feeding the parts of yourself that are self-seeking, unhealthy, and self-satisfying and learn to trust God. Galatians 6:8 says, "Those who live only to satisfy their own sinful nature will harvest decay and death from that sinful nature. But those who live to please the Spirit will harvest everlasting life from the Spirit." Every time you try to rationalize things to make yourself feel better about going after your own natural cravings and desires, those actions only result in corruption. Focus your time and energy on feeding the spiritual side of your life. You can easily convince yourself that certain relationships and activities are okay, but if they're centered on feeding the flesh, nothing good is going to come of it. Make sure that your decisions and actions are not motivated by the flesh. Pray about situations before just running after your feelings. Don't make big decisions when you're emotional. Never neglect the godly, spiritual side of yourself.

Learn to discern within when you are motivated by your flesh and when you are motivated by the Spirit of God. Galatians 5:24 explains, "Those who belong to Christ Jesus have nailed the passions and desires of their sinful nature to his cross and crucified them there." Trust me, God's ways are always better than following our human fleshly ways. Encounters with Him are more satisfying than anything else. Trust me.

2. THE ENEMY AND SIN

Romans 7:15-20 says, "I don't really understand myself, for I want to do what is right, but I don't do it. Instead, I do what I hate. But if I know that what I am doing is wrong, this shows that I agree that the law is good. So, I am not the one doing wrong; it is sin living in me that does it. And I know that nothing good lives in me, that is, in my sinful nature. I want to do what is right, but I can't. I want to do what is good, but I don't. I don't want to do what is wrong, but I do it anyway. But if I do what I don't want to do, I am not really the one doing wrong; it is sin living in me that does it."

Make a decision to turn away from everything in your life that you know for a fact is displeasing to God. Confess any sin that is at work in you and believe in the power of the blood of Jesus to wash and cleanse you as white as snow (Isaiah 1:18). The Bible says the enemy comes to kill, steal, and destroy (John 10:10). Satan never wants you to be what God's Word says you are. He knows that if you ever live out your God-purpose, you will be another soldier of light aggressively defeating his kingdom of darkness. The enemy could care less about you. He does not attack you because he has a bone to pick with you. He is only concerned with attacking God's will. This is why Jesus said to pray that God's Kingdom come and His will would be done on earth as it is in heaven (Matthew 6:9-13), because the resistance and the fight of the enemy is against God's will and Kingdom coming to earth through us as it is in heaven. This battle is not yours; it's the Lord's (2 Chronicles 20:15). There is a spiritual battle between the Kingdom of Darkness and the Kingdom of Light. So, every attack that you have ever experienced in your life has actually been to prevent or hinder God's will from manifesting through you.

Whenever you knowingly sin and go against what you know to be right (James 4:27), you give permission to the enemy to bully you, bring darkness in, torment, and hinder you. He wants to block your God-given purpose. Romans 6:16 explains, "Don't you realize that you become the slave of whatever you choose to obey? You can be a slave to sin, which leads to death, or you can choose to obey God, which leads to righteous living." This is why you can't afford to play around with sin. As you sin, you yield and open yourself to the enemy and his attacks. You will learn more about the tactics of the enemy and how to fight in later chapters.

You may feel like with the family you were born into, you didn't have a fighting chance to have a healthy upbringing and keep sin out of your life. Sometimes there are cycles in family lines that repeat themselves. An example of this is cancer that travels in the DNA of families and is passed down. Or, a grandmother, mother, and daughter that were all sexually abused or all formed drug addictions. These are examples of family curses and demonic assignments that can be broken through Jesus. You do not have to be a product of the toxic and painful cycles and mindsets of your family. I declare over you that not only will you break the power of sin in your life, but you will be the one who breaks generational curses, sins, illness, and toxic cycles for your family and children in Jesus' name (Exodus 34:7; Deuteronomy 30:19; Ezekiel 18:1-4).

If you know that you have sin in your life right now, or generational curses at work, that opened the door to the enemy, pray a prayer of repentance. You can stand in the gap and repent on behalf of your generational lines to break the curses and toxic cycles, to cut off and cease the attacks and assaults of the enemy. No longer will you be victimized by the enemy, but the enemy will be victimized by Christ in you, the hope of Glory! There are prayer points at the conclusion of the Self-Work section at the end of this chapter to lead you through that. You are now part of God's family and you get to receive the identity and inheritance that belongs to you through Him. God's redeeming love is aggressive. He will be all that you never had and fill every relational void in your life.

3. THE WORLD

Romans 12:2 encourages us, "Don't copy the behavior and customs of this world, but let God transform you into a new person by changing the way you think. Then you will learn to know God's will for you, which is good and pleasing and perfect."

This does not mean that you have to isolate yourself and never interact with the world. In fact, you are supposed to be in the world, but not a part of the world. There is a difference between being relevant and on-trend with culture, and being worldly.

You will never match up to the world's standard. The world is full of temptation, and it is trying to make you forget that you are a citizen of the Kingdom of God. This world is not your home. The enemy will try to show you all of the kingdoms of the world to make it seem easier than the path that God has for you. He tempted Jesus that way (Matthew 4) and the Bible says a servant is no greater than their master (John 13:16). Satan tried to offer all the worldly kingdoms to Jesus if He would bow down and worship him. When we choose worldly things and ways, we literally put them before God. First John 2:15-16 says, "Do not love this world nor the things it offers you, for when you love the world, you do not have the love of the Father in you. For the world offers only a craving for physical pleasure, a craving for everything we see, and pride in our achievements and possessions. These are not from the Father, but are from this world." James 4:4 continues, "You adulterers! Don't you realize that friendship with the world makes you an enemy of God? I say it again: If you want to be a friend of the world, you make yourself an enemy of God."

4. THE PAST

Your past does not determine your future. I'm totally an example of that. You absolutely must find a way to let go of everything from your past. Forgive yourself, forgive others, and forgive God for any hard feelings toward Him from your past. In the next chapter, you will learn how to forgive and release people who have hurt you in the past. Psalm 71:20 gives us this insight: "You have allowed me to suffer much hardship, but you will restore me to life again and lift me up from the depths of the earth." Your past can never be too messed up for God to transform! Don't allow the negative things of your past to control your present and give you anxiety about your future. Live "in the now." In order to be everything that God has purposed you to be, you can't hold on to the shame, condemnation, and guilt of the past. It's time to move forward in Jesus' name.

5. REPLACING LIES WITH TRUTH

One of the biggest parts of your transformation is the renewing of your mind, the way you think. You must renew your mind with the Word and Truth that He longs to reveal to you through personal encounter. It is the mind-renewing process that reveals what God's perfect will is for you. God wants to transform the way you think. Often people who have painful or traumatic situations in the past learn things from those experiences that aren't true, but feel very real.

For example, because of the sexual abuse in my childhood, I believed the lies that I was dirty, unlovable, and unprotected. That violation and physical abuse would always continue happening to me. God had to teach me His truths because those lies felt real. I listened to sermons and got advice from many, but personal revelation in the Word and God-encounters is what made the Truth become real deep down inside. I had to have heavenly experiences to override the demonic experiences that taught me the lies.

Lies that we learn from trauma are anchored in our soul and become the lens through which we process situations, until a higher reality of truth is revealed—not in head knowledge, but in the reality of your heart. If there are core lies that are part of the way that you filter and think about people and circumstances, then it's time to know the Truth. Sometimes this is the very reason for sin cycles that seem to be unbreakable. There is a root lie that causes you to devalue yourself and feel like it's normal or "the way things are." What do you really believe deep down inside? Ask God, "What lies am I believing? What truth do You want to reveal to me?" Record them in the self-work section of this chapter.

Romans 8:28 says, "And we know that God causes everything to work together for the good of those who love God and are called according to his purpose for them." There is nothing that you've ever done or has been done to you that can't be turned around into something good. I have experienced this and I live this. Everything that I've been through, as horrible and traumatic as my life has been, is now a powerful tool to demonstrate how real God is and to point people to Jesus Christ.

I shouldn't be alive or sane after everything I've endured, but I am proof that God is real and I feel privileged to be a real witness of what God can do. My past has qualified me to help others because I've lived what they've lived and felt what they have felt. My scars have given me authority to help heal others. There are things about your past that maybe you've thought you could never get over, but even those deep, secret hurting places can be healed and used to help pull others out of the same pain and bondage.

Don't allow memories of the things you've experienced to torment you and hinder you from moving forward and succeeding in life. Whatever you can't let go of still has power over you! Isn't it crazy how one damaging person, action, or situation can determine how we feel about ourselves and our lives? You cannot give any one person or event in time that much control over you. Learn to let go and allow God to put back together all of the broken pieces of the past. He will make you brand new again!

I want to encourage you. You are alive today. You must be confident and comfortable in the person God created you to be and the purpose you were destined to fulfill on the earth. Make a commitment to God and to yourself that you are going to do whatever it takes to yield and remain in relationship with the Lord. It's going to be a journey. It may be hard. You will have to fight for it, but your eternal rewards will outweigh any struggles or hardships along the way.

SELF-WORK

This simple exercise is to help you have an awareness of your natural and spiritual space. Once you recognize unhealthy people, activities, places, and thoughts, it will be easier to break away from those things and replace them with the healthy, positive, and godly. Be honest with yourself and use this as an opportunity to speed up your transformation process. Turn away from everything that can hinder you. Embrace everything that can encourage you and will propel you forward into your God-given destiny. Ask the Lord to reveal these things to you.

NEGATIVE PEOPLE

_____
_____
_____
_____
_____

POSITIVE PEOPLE

_____
_____
_____
_____
_____

NEGATIVE ACTIVITIES

_____
_____
_____
_____
_____
_____

POSITIVE ACTIVITIES

_____
_____
_____
_____
_____
_____

NEGATIVE PLACES

_____
_____
_____
_____
_____
_____

POSITIVE PLACES

_____
_____
_____
_____
_____
_____

NEGATIVE THOUGHTS (LIES)

_____
_____
_____
_____
_____
_____

POSITIVE THOUGHTS (TRUTH)

_____
_____
_____
_____
_____
_____

TRANSFORMATION PRAYER

Father God,

- I enter Your gates with thanksgiving and your courts with praise. (Psalm 100:4)
- I choose to forgive and release those who have sinned against me. (Matt. 18:21-35)
- I repent of all sin, transgressions, and iniquity. (Acts 3:19)
- I repent of all word curses, vows, judgments, and accusations that I have spoken against myself or others. (Prov. 6:2; James 5:9; Rom. 2:1; Prov. 18:20-21; Matt. 7:1-5; Luke 6:37-42; James 3:4-5)
- I repent for all ungodly soul ties. I cut off all demonic

attacks that have come into my life from ungodly soul ties in Jesus' name. (1 Corinthians 6:16)
- I stand in the gap for my generational lines and I repent for all sin, transgression, iniquity, curses, agreements, and contracts with the enemy on my father's and mother's (and step-parents') family lines. I break all demonic assignments and generational curses in Jesus' name. I apply the blood of Jesus over my family.
- I ask that You lift any veils off of my eyes and heart, any places where I have been blinded by lies or wounds, that I may have clear revelation of truth. Give me ears to hear what the Spirit of the Lord is saying. (2 Cor. 3:14-15; Mark 4:9; Ephesians 1:17)
- Father God, I ask that You cancel every accusation against me in Jesus' name, according to Colossians 2:13-15 as I declare this Scripture over my life: "You were dead because of your sins and because your sinful nature was not yet cut away. Then God made you alive with Christ, for he forgave all our sins. He canceled the record of the charges against us and took it away by nailing it to the cross. In this way, he disarmed the spiritual rulers and authorities. He shamed them publicly by his victory over them on the cross."
- Holy Spirit, I ask that You heal and remove all of my emotional pain from the past. Wash over and deactivate every trigger that causes emotional distress, pain, sickness, fear, or anxiety in Jesus' name.
- I ask that You give me wisdom. "For I will give you a mouth and a wisdom which all of your adversaries will not be able to contradict or resist." (Luke 21:15)
- I declare that I am the righteousness of Christ. (2 Cor. 5:21)

- I declare that I am seated in heavenly places in Christ. (Ephes. 2:6)
- I declare that I am not under the authority or the dominion of the kingdom of darkness, but I have been transferred into the Kingdom of Jesus. (Col. 1:13-14)
- I declare that I am a royalty in God's family. (Rev. 1:5-6; Rom. 8:15; 1 Pet. 2:9)
- Father God, heal me, transform me, and deliver me.

I ask all of these things in Jesus' mighty name, amen!

2.3 THE RECOVERY_

If you have ever been through something difficult, this chapter is for you. When you experience traumatic events in life that you don't confront—even though you may think sweeping it under the rug solves the problem—it doesn't. There is spiritual, emotional, and mental freedom that God wants you to experience. Your present and future life will be more successful and purposeful when you heal the areas that could be holding you back or causing you to make poor decisions on your life's journey.

One of the biggest lies the enemy tells people going through a healing process is, "It's going to take forever!" He will whisper to you that it will take years of recovery, many twelve-step programs, and lots of counseling to work through your hurt and brokenness from the past. The enemy will try to make you feel like there is no hope for your situation and that you will never truly be free from the hurt and issues of your past. This is not true! Yes, sometimes recovery can be a long journey, but it doesn't always have to be. One of my favorite stories in the Bible is found in Mark chapter 5. A crazy, demon-possessed man has a spiritual confrontation with Jesus that changed his life forever. He experienced recovery in one encounter with the Lord.

Mark 5:1-6 says, "So they arrived at the other side of the lake, in the region of the Gerasene. When Jesus climbed out of the boat, a man possessed by an evil spirit came out from a cemetery to meet him. This man lived among the burial caves and could no longer be restrained, even with a chain. Whenever he was put into chains and shackles— as he often was—he snapped the chains from his wrists and smashed the shackles. No one was strong enough to subdue him. Day and night he wandered among the burial caves and in the hills, howling and cutting himself with sharp stones. When Jesus was still some distance away, the man saw him, ran to meet him, and bowed low before him."

This man was crazy, naked, aggressive, an outcast, and if you read on, you'll see he happened to be possessed with thousands of demons. No counselor could help him. Not his mom or dad, his friends, law enforcement, not the religion of the region (idol worship)—nothing could free him from his pain. No one was able to help him. He was hopeless. Now if it would take anyone a lifetime to recover, it would be this man. If you are in your right mind enough to be reading this book, I can safely assume that you are in a much better condition than he was! In one moment at the feet of Jesus, he was completely set free, saved, clothed, and restored to his right mind. If Jesus could help, cure, save, and deliver this insane demoniac, then He can do the same for you. If He could transform me and give me a brand-new, purpose-filled life, then He can absolutely do it for you! God is no respecter of persons (Acts 10:34); this means that whenever you see Him do something for someone else, it is totally possible for Him to do the same thing for you.

Emotionally, there are some things that you can do in your healing process that are very liberating. The Self-Work at the conclusion of chapters 2.1 and 2.2 are extremely important. You must change your self-talk to what the Word says about you. Embrace the positives in your life and eliminate the negatives. I would like to add a few more elements: spending time with Jesus, a total surrender to God, forgiveness toward all, and confronting every hidden thing.

TIME WITH JESUS

The demoniac mentioned in Mark 5 spent time with Jesus and this resulted in his freedom. He also received his purpose for living. He evangelized the region for Jesus after finding freedom through time spent with Him. You do this by spending time in the Word; Jesus is the Word wrapped in flesh (John 1). Spend time in God's presence because "the Lord is the Spirit, and wherever the Spirit of the Lord is, there is freedom" (2 Corinthians 3:17). Talk to Him. Develop a stronger prayer life. The more you get to know Him and the more time you spend with Him, the more freedom you will experience. Reading His Word should not be boring. In fact, it can be adventurous and full of encounters. If you lean into the Bible as you read it, asking Holy Spirit to make it real to you, sometimes you can literally see, hear, feel, touch, and taste the reality of the Word.

When you catch a real personal revelation of what Jesus did for you on the cross and everything you now have through the grace of God, every hurt and sin of your life will literally melt away. I know for a fact that without the freedom I received from Jesus, I would have been dead a long time ago. We can cast all of our worries and anxieties on Him because He cares for us (1 Peter 5:7). There is no way that I could live with all of my guilt, trauma, and shame. Without Jesus, I would still be a sexually abused, bipolar, raped, beaten, drug-and-alcohol-loving, abortion-having stripper and sex trafficking victim. God helped me to let go of all of that and throw it off of my life onto Him. Over 2,000 years ago, He took care of it all on the cross! You don't have to continue carrying all of the pain and shame of your life. Give your heaviness, stress, confusion, negative thoughts, and painful feelings to

Jesus. He has been waiting for you to spend some quality time with Him so that He can completely heal and deliver you.

Vent to Him. Don't air out all your feelings on social media to anyone who will listen! Whenever you are going through something, before you tell anybody, tell Jesus first. If He is the Lord of your life, then you should go to Him first with everything. Let me go a step further: the only "few" people you should confide in should be those who have a life surrendered to Jesus. He or she must be someone that can actually help you and pray for you. The more people, things, and places you reach out to for help—other than Jesus—the messier and more confusing your recovery process will become.

You don't need personal opinions and man's advice; you need Jesus. There has to be a hunger in you to truly spend time with Him. Every time there is an altar call, run to Jesus and be the first one at His feet. Every time you feel Him stirring in your heart during praise and worship, don't hold back... embrace the presence of God and press into Him with all you've got! When you are going to bed with tears in your eyes, focus your heart and mind on Jesus and allow Him to minister to you. Every opportunity you get, run to Him.

TOTAL SURENDER

A very simple, yet powerful statement that I heard somebody say is, "God is God and you are not." We have to stop trying to be in control of our lives. Stop trying to fix yourself. Stop trying to fix others. Allow God to be the God of your life because nobody can fix like Him! If you want to be completely free and empowered to accomplish something great in this life, you have to give up control and totally surrender to Him.

That was the moment my life radically changed. I was tired of trying to do everything my way. It wasn't working and I just got myself into bigger and bigger messes. I finally came to the point of surrender. I didn't care if I had to live in a cardboard box, I just wanted to be living out the plan God had for me.

Being in God's will is better than all of the riches in the world; I can say that because I personally know this to be true. Thirty-thousand-dollar shopping sprees were pointless to me when I was mentally tormented and had no peace. What good is it to look like you have it all together on the outside if you are wounded and struggling within? I've been there.

I've come to find that when a person tries to control his or her own life, really it means that person does not trust God enough. It's a trust issue. Many times, when something bad happened in my life, instead of running to God and staying in a place of surrender, I ran from God and took matters into my own hands. I actually blamed God when bad things happened and said things like, "How could You let this happen to me, God? Why me? How could You do this to me?" In my moment of "real" surrender, I had a revelation: it was never God doing those horrible things to me! God is a good God. It was actually the enemy attacking my life because he never wanted me to know who I am and fulfill God's plan on this earth. So all that time, I blamed God and didn't trust that He could actually help me out of my situation when it was really the enemy to blame! Whenever I started doing good and getting closer to God, I would get attacked in some way, then blame it on God, take my trust back, and run away from Him to try to fix it all by myself.

A surrendered life trusts God no matter what and remains unmovable. Before I surrendered to God, I didn't know how to fight the enemy when those attacks came. (I know now and will teach you in a later chapter.) The place of surrender is a powerful position! You can't fight your battles like God can. You can't heal and deliver yourself like God can. You can't empower yourself like God can. You can't give yourself victory and joy like God can. Get the point? God can do everything better than you because He is God and you are not! When you totally surrender, it actually becomes fun to trust in God. There will be situations that arise and you'll find yourself saying, "God, I don't know how I'm going to get out of this situation, but it will be fun to watch You figure it out. I trust You!" Let God be in control. Trust me, He's much better at controlling your life than you.

THE FORGIVENESS TRAIN

1. FORGIVE YOURSELF

Is there any area of your life where you are still condemning yourself? Are there Scriptural truths that you know are true in your mind, but don't feel true about you in your heart? For example, if you know God loves you in your head, but in your heart, you feel unlovable and unworthy, then there are some things you need to forgive yourself for.

It is so dangerous to not forgive yourself. Basically, a lack of forgiving self means you do not believe that Jesus' death on the cross was good enough for God to wash away all of your sins. If the blood of Jesus is powerful enough to cause God to forgive you, then it should be enough for you to let go of your sins of the past and forgive yourself. If God looks at you as brand new and squeaky clean, then that should be how you see yourself. It's easy to believe the lies of condemnation from the enemy that say, "I don't deserve any blessings from God because I know what I've done." All of that stinking thinking has to go! You have to forgive yourself and receive everything by grace that comes with being a child of God. If it's good enough for God, it has to be good enough for you! No one on this planet is greater than God, but when you allow feelings of unworthiness and unforgiveness to rule your thinking, you're actually saying that you are greater than God. A servant is no greater than his master (John 13:16). So when something is good enough for God, but not good enough for you, in reality, you make yourself bigger than God. Forgive yourself!

Think about Jesus dying on the cross for your sins. How many times would your Savior have to die on the cross to make you satisfied enough to forgive yourself? Ask God to help you completely forgive yourself of everything you've ever done: every bad decision, every horrible relationship, every sin, every selfish action, every time you hurt your family or people close to you... all of it! When you truthfully forgive yourself, you will no longer keep record of the wrongs you've done. You will know that God has completely erased your past sins, made them as white as snow, thrown them into the depths of the ocean, and removed them as far as the east is from the west away from you. This is how you are to look at yourself. God's forgiveness is the same forgiveness we are to forgive ourselves with. That is freedom!

2. FORGIVE OTHERS

Forgiving someone is more for you than it is for the person you are forgiving. When you don't forgive others, it can also affect your personal relationship with God. In order to keep your heart and life pure, you must forgive. Matthew 6:15 says, "But if you refuse to forgive others, your Father will not forgive your sins." This is a huge part of your recovery process, because if you can't forgive those who hurt you in the past, then they still have control over you. More importantly, they have control over God's forgiveness toward you. When you don't forgive others, you allow them to impact your relationship with God. I'm just clarifying what the Word says. That person still controls your thoughts and emotions as you replay the event over and over in your mind throughout life. As you do that, all of the negative feelings associated with what they did come back every time you think about them or see them. Don't you want to be free from that?

Forgiving others is truly supernatural. You may not "feel" like forgiving them, but you can "choose" to forgive them, which is bringing your will in alignment. It is not normal for me to have completely forgiven the people who raped me, abused me, trafficked me, beat me... it is not normal! But with God's help and with His supernatural forgiving power, I have forgiven everyone who has hurt me. I am no longer their victim! Memories of what they did to me have no power to haunt me anymore.

Most of the time, the people who hurt others just move on with their lives, but those hurt by them live with the scars and constant reminders of the pain inflicted upon them. It doesn't even affect the person who hurt you anymore; in fact, they probably could care less. Unforgiveness keeps that situation in the present for you, even though it may have happened a long time ago. The memories of what they did, struggles relationally with others, the anger, sadness, anxiety, nightmares, emotional triggers, and pain remain. You still carry the weight of what they did to you when you don't forgive. If you're still living with these things, forgiveness will be major in setting you free from the hurt and the pain of your past. When you forgive, the enemy can't continually use the past to torment your present.

Not only do we need to forgive, but we need to release the individual from what they owe us. For example, you can forgive a parent for something they did to you, but if you have an expectation that they owe you an apology or to be a healthy positive parent in your life, they may not know how to do that. They do owe you as a parent to be kind and loving, but if that debt, that expectation, is still owed, then every time they fail to be that for you, the wound or offense will still be there. You would still feel broken or stuck because something that rightfully belongs to you has not been given. You have to FORGIVE them for the painful things they've done and RELEASE them from what they owe you. In the following Scripture, Jesus explains.

> "Then Peter came to him and asked, 'Lord, how often should I forgive someone who sins against me? Seven times?' 'No, not seven times,' Jesus replied, 'but seventy times seven! Therefore, the Kingdom of Heaven can be compared to a king who decided to bring his accounts up to date with servants who had

borrowed money from him. In the process, one of his debtors was brought in who owed him millions of dollars. He couldn't pay, so his master ordered that he be sold—along with his wife, his children, and everything he owned—to pay the debt.

'But the man fell down before his master and begged him, 'Please, be patient with me, and I will pay it all.' Then his master was filled with pity for him, and he released him and forgave his debt.

'But when the man left the king, he went to a fellow servant who owed him a few thousand dollars. He grabbed him by the throat and demanded instant payment.

'His fellow servant fell down before him and begged for a little more time. 'Be patient with me, and I will pay it,' he pleaded. But his creditor wouldn't wait. He had the man arrested and put in prison until the debt could be paid in full.

'When some of the other servants saw this, they were very upset. They went to the king and told him everything that had happened. Then the king called in the man he had forgiven and said, 'You evil servant! I forgave you that tremendous debt because you pleaded with me. Shouldn't you have mercy on your fellow servant, just as I had mercy on you?' Then the angry king sent the man to prison to be tortured until he had paid his entire debt.

'That's what my heavenly Father will do to you if you refuse to forgive your brothers and sisters from your heart.'"

(Matthew 18:21-35 NLT)

Unforgiveness can be a trick of the enemy to keep you in a jail of torment and to hold you back from moving forward in your God-purpose and life-calling. Matthew 5:23-24 says, "So if you are presenting a sacrifice at the altar in the Temple and you suddenly remember that someone has something against you, leave your sacrifice there at the altar. Go and be reconciled to that person. Then come and offer your sacrifice to God." Obedience is better than sacrifice and God tells us to forgive others, be forgiven by others, and clear up any offenses. So, you could be sacrificing your whole life for God and giving all that you can in worship, finances, and service, but if you have unresolved unforgiveness issues with people, then God would prefer that you stop and make all that junk right first.

Sometimes the enemy will persuade people to do things to you just to tempt you into unforgiveness, because he knows that is one sure way to hinder the work that God desires to do through your life. Don't fall into the temptation of offense! You can't afford to allow people to bother you to the point of being offended. I prayed for a woman with epilepsy to receive a healing miracle, and nothing was happening. I heard Holy Spirit say, "Ask her if there is anyone she needs to forgive." As I did, she broke down in tears and chose to forgive the person the Lord highlighted to her. We prayed again for healing in Jesus' name and the symptoms of her condition left, as well as some pain she had in her body. She was able to test it out by holding her head back a certain way that would previously throw her into seizures. She was completely healed and the key was forgiveness. You must let it go—if someone really angers or hurts you, immediately ask God for help to forgive and for wisdom about how to clear the offense. Don't let it just fester and build.

One of the things that helped me to forgive others is trying to look at them through God's eyes. The people who sexually abused me in my childhood never grew up with the dream of becoming pedophiles. Something happened to them that caused them to be broken and confused enough to allow the enemy to use them. I had to learn how to separate the person from the demonic force using that person. Then I was able to, in a weird way, actually feel sorry for the people who abused me. I understand the Lord's statement, "Forgive them because they know not what they do." As a child growing up in life, I'm sure they never thought in all of their innocence, "I want to grow up to be a monster and sexually abuse children." There is a backstory and a reason why every criminal becomes a criminal. They were a victim of something at some point in their life that caused them to be this way. This thought may be difficult for many people to understand, but it helped me to forgive and let go. I actually pray that every person who violated my body and every person who ever harmed me finds Jesus and experiences salvation and deliverance from their own hurts and demons.

Certainly, there are some situations in which it would not be wise or safe to go to a person to try and talk things through to forgiveness. If someone has sexually abused you or physically harmed you, you obviously shouldn't take a trip to their house to have a one-on-one conversation. However, it is possible for God to help you forgive those people. In the Self-Work section at the conclusion of this chapter, there is an exercise to help you get started forgiving.

3. FORGIVE GOD

Without even realizing it, we can blame God for things that we experience and it affects our relationship with Him. As I previously mentioned, earlier in life when I would experience traumatic events, I ran from God instead of to Him. I would say, "How could you let this happen to me, God? Why me? I was doing my best to serve You and You didn't protect me!?" Bitterness and resentment can creep in toward God when we are going through trying situations.

One of the greatest revelations of my life was when I realized that God is good, perfect, and holy in all of His ways. It was never God doing those horrible things to me, but the enemy. I was casting my anger and blame in the wrong direction. I was projecting feelings about the men in my life onto God. This may be a surprising thought that you need to forgive God. Is there anything in your life that you have blamed God for? Have you ever run away from God feeling that He caused or allowed issues in your life? Do you view Father God like you view your earthly father? God is NOT like man, but we can feel that way when man has rejected, wounded, violated, or abandoned us, because it's what we are used to. His ways are so much higher than man's. God will not hurt you, leave you, or speak harshly toward you. Furthermore, ask God to forgive you for having such a distorted perspective of Him. The reality is that God is the only answer to all of your issues and hurts. We sometimes have to relearn what we think we know about God, even if we've been Christians for a long time. I encourage you to spend some time in the Word and in prayer asking God to show you who He really is all over again.

CONFRONT

God can't heal what you're not willing to confront. You have to be real with yourself and Him. Are there any closed off rooms or compartments of your life that you just don't want to look into? Are you someone who would prefer to sweep things under the rug? You must allow God to renew every area of your life. You should want to be whole spiritually, mentally, and emotionally. This doesn't mean that you have to live in your past and relive everything that you've ever been through, but there is power in confronting and confessing those things before God and allowing Him to bring healing and deliverance.

If you have severe trauma in your past and there are some suppressed memories, don't feel bad if you can't remember. Sometimes events were so traumatizing that the Lord allowed them to be suppressed or fractured so that you could survive. Don't feel shame and pressure to re-live anything. Just ask Jesus to bring up the things that He knows you're ready to remember. Sometimes He conceals and heals things in His grace toward us. He will be right there with you. He is so faithful, gentle, and loving in the middle of healing from trauma.

Journaling is a wonderful way to emotionally and mentally process things. Journal everything you feel that you've never allowed God to heal and deliver you of. Talk to the Lord as you write, then pray after you're finished. The Holy Spirit will be your comforter (John 14:16); allow Jesus to be your Prince of Peace, bringing peace into every area of your life (Isaiah 9:6).

Spend one-on-one time with Jesus. Surrender all control of your life to God. Forgive yourself. Forgive others. Forgive God. Confront and confess everything to Him. These are the basics of recovery.

Spend time doing the Self-Work section below and ask God to help you through your recovery process. Don't allow the memories of the things you've experienced to torment you and hinder you from moving forward and succeeding in life. Whatever you can't let go of still has power over you. Isn't it crazy how one damaging person, action, or situation can determine how we feel about ourselves and our lives? You can't give any one person or event in time that much control! Learn to let go and allow God to heal all of the broken pieces of the past. He will make you brand new again.

SELF-WORK

Ask God these questions and wait for His answer.

Father God, what areas of my life do You need me to surrender to You (i.e. finances, love relationship, children)?

_____
_____
_____
_____
_____

Father God, what do I need to forgive myself for?

_____
_____
_____
_____
_____
_____

Father God, who do I need to forgive and release?

_____
_____
_____
_____
_____
_____

Father God, how have these people and what they did to me affected me today?

_____
_____
_____
_____
_____
_____

Father God, is there anything that I need to forgive You for? Anything that I have been blaming You for? What is the truth about who You are to me? Give me a pure perspective of You.

_____
_____
_____
_____
_____
_____

Father God, what areas of my life have I never confronted, confessed, or allowed You to heal?

_____
_____
_____
_____
_____
_____

(Spend time journaling these things out on a separate piece of paper.)

2.4 THE "YES"

"'For I know the plans I have for you,' says the Lord. 'They are plans for good and not for disaster, to give you a future and a hope.'" (Jeremiah 29:11)

Discovering God's specific, individual purpose for your life is an extremely fun journey! We have discussed the general role of every Christian. Now let's use a magnifying glass to "zero in" on key things in your life that will reveal what God wants to do through you as an individual.

ASK AND LISTEN

First things first... have you prayed and asked God what your specific purpose is? As a child of God, He wants you to know His voice. Open communication with Him is part of the divine relationship He desires to have with you. Hearing the voice of God is yet another benefit of the Lord Jesus dying on the cross for our sins. The moment Jesus committed His spirit into the hands of God and died, the veil of the temple was torn (Matthew 27:51). Prior to this, people had to generally do everything through a priest. The average person did not have the liberty of hearing

God's voice all the time and freely being able to come boldly before the throne of grace (Hebrews 4:16). Thanks to Jesus, that veil in the temple that separated us from intimacy with Him was torn and now we can have a close relationship with God. Jeremiah 29:13 encourages us, "If you look for me wholeheartedly, you will find me."

God does not want to play guessing games with you. The Bible says He is not the author of confusion (1 Corinthians 14:33). God wants you to be able to clearly hear and understand His voice. Pray and ask God to give you ears to hear what the Spirit of the Lord is saying to you (Matthew 13:9). The following Scripture has a promise within it that you can pray if you are having difficulty hearing Him.

John 10:4-5 says, "After he has gathered his own flock, he walks ahead of them, and they follow him because they know his voice. They won't follow a stranger; they will run from him because they don't know his voice."

Jesus was saying that it is possible to know His voice, follow Him, and choose to NOT follow a stranger, the enemy. This gives hope to people struggling with being bombarded by the voices of the enemy. I once struggled with severe mental illness and there were so many voices in my head, lies, and self-sabotaging thoughts. Jesus was so faithful to reveal to me what voices were demonic attacks and what voice was HIS. He gave me discernment to "know" His voice and He empowered me to make the conscious choice to no longer follow the pressures, torment, and promptings of the demonic, the "strangers." In knowing Jesus, He helps us with every area of our lives.

Another encouraging Scripture that ties in with the power of free will to choose God over the verbal assaults of the enemy is found in James 4:7. The verse says, "So humble yourselves before God. Resist the devil, and he will flee from you." We must submit and humble ourselves before God and then we have the power to resist the enemy and his confusing lies. But we do have to

RESIST the enemy. Keep resisting the temptations and lies of the enemy in order to be free, stay free, and follow the voice of the Lord.

When struggling to hear God's voice, sometimes our problem is that during prayer time, we do all the talking and we ask God lots of questions and then say, "Amen." It's as though you were calling someone on the phone and talking to them, asking them big questions and then suddenly saying, "Bye!" and hanging up before giving him or her a chance to answer. It is imperative that you spend some time waiting for God to respond. Prayer is not supposed to be a one-way conversation. When you talk to the Lord, be aware that there are several ways that you may get a response. You could hear His voice through a vision, dream, impression, trance, discernment, tangible encounter of His Presence and Glory, etc. Sometimes people feel like they don't hear God, but He gives them visions and pictures that they dismiss as they strain to "hear." Be open to all of the ways that God can speak to you. It's so much fun!

Don't you know that the One who created you wants you to know why you were created? Ask, then listen and wait upon the Lord. If you're new to listening, you may have to eliminate all distractions by turning off the TV, putting your phone on silent, clearing all of your busy thoughts, and just start listening. As you spend more time listening to the voice of God and reading the Word of God, you will not only learn who you are and your reason for existence, but you will learn who God is. You were created in His image (Genesis 1:27). Your identity is defined in God's image. Getting to know the very personality and characteristics of God will help you discover yourself in ways you never knew were possible.

The following is an exercise you can use to hear God for the first time or to sharpen your ability to open your spiritual eyes and ears to consistently hear from Him. Get a blank journal and commit to spending some of your prayer time clearing your thoughts and just listening and watching. Ask questions like, "Father what do You want to say to me and what do You want to show me?" Make sure to document what you hear, see, or feel and find Scriptures that align with what you've just encountered. God will NEVER speak something that is contrary to His Word.

If you are seeing visions for the first time, you may see a color, a number, or a prophetic symbol like an animal or a type of building. Do a Bible study of the symbols and discover an amazing sermon of revelation tailored just for you. I love the prophetic symbolic language of God in visions, trances, and dreams. It is so adventurous to explore the meaning of these symbols which require more conversation with Him for the interpretation. When I was first learning how to interpret these things, I would record it in my journal, highlight all of the symbols, and take note of my feelings toward those symbols (i.e. happy, unsure, good, bad). Then I would look up Scriptures that have those symbols in them and write the Scriptures that Holy Spirit revealed aligned. Then I would have a beautiful detailed message straight from the heart of God to me. I still to this day record my encounters to steward them well.

If you are hearing His voice for the first time, God may speak something to you that seems very simple at first like, "I love you." No matter how simple it may seem, search the Scriptures and try to understand what His message to you really means. Studying God's love is one of the most powerful and liberating things that anyone could seek to know more about. God's words to you personally will absolutely change your life! The more you know God, the more you know yourself.

Philippians 3:10 (AMP) says, "For my determined purpose is that I may know Him that I may progressively become more deeply and intimately acquainted with Him, perceiving and recognizing and understanding the wonders of His Person more strongly and more clearly."

REVELATION AND CONFIRMATION

When God spoke to my husband John that he was to marry me, John asked God to confirm it to him. The next day, a total stranger walked up to him in the library and asked, "Are you a Christian leader? Would you understand what it meant if I gave you a word?" John responded, "Yes." She continued, "God sent me here to tell you that you know who your wife is–yes–that is she and don't worry about anything. God will bring her to you." Let's not overlook the fact that God can also speak to you through an angelic encounter. It happened all over the Bible!

I can honestly say that every major life decision pertaining to my God-purpose was confirmed to me in ways that were undeniable. As I previously mentioned, when God called me, He sent several people to speak over my life and confirm it. God knows you personally and knows how to get your attention through revelation and confirmation. It may not be exactly the same way that He confirms His will to others. God wants to be very personal with you; He will make your purpose clear to you so you will be 100% sure of it.

There will come a time, if it hasn't come yet, that you will get a very clear revelation of a specific task, assignment, ministry, business, or cause that you are to pursue. You will know without a shadow of a doubt. Remember, it's not God's will for you to be confused and guessing; everyone on earth has a purpose! It may not be full-time ministry from a pulpit. Your purpose may be to work a secular job and use your gifts and talents in that area to help fund the spreading of the Gospel. You may be called to impact politics, the business world, the education system, or the entertainment industry. God wants to be involved in every area of society, not just in the Church. If every Christian was only called to work in ministry in a church building, what would our world look like? A whole lot worse! Open your mind to the fact that we are all ministers sent out into the world to accomplish things for

God. Our feet should be prepared and ready to spread the Gospel of peace (Ephesians 6:15) wherever God leads us.

If your passion and gift is photography, maybe you will be able to travel the world on missions trips, capturing God-moments that will be used to help fund missionary work in the world. You may be a business owner who starts a program to donate items to the needy on a monthly basis, sharing the message of love and hope. You may be a computer-techy type who can use your skills and talent to help ministries with their graphics, videos, website, marketing, and branding. The examples can go on and on, but the point is that no matter what you're passionate about and gifted in, God can use it to fulfill the Great Commission in some way. Pray and ask God to give you wisdom to make your time and energy effective in His desire to see souls saved.

Once God makes your purpose clear to you and you become comfortable with it, get to work A.S.A.P. Increased passion for ministry comes when lives are changed as a result of your effort and God's work through you. Don't hesitate or procrastinate in doing God's business. Accept the calling and assignment of God on your life; be confident in your purpose and obedient to the revelation and confirmation of what you are to complete during your lifetime.

EMBRACE THE ROAD AHEAD

This journey with God is incredible! The greatest joy is being with Him in the journey, total devotion, adoration, and being present with Him through every part of the process. Once you accept the calling on your life, it's important that you don't begin overthinking! When we try and figure out every detail, we will most likely start leaning on our own understanding, which is not wise. Proverbs 3:5-7 admonishes us, "Trust in the Lord with all your heart; do not depend on your own understanding. Seek his will in all you do, and he will show you which path to take. Don't be impressed with your own wisdom. Instead, fear the Lord and turn away from evil."

Begin to trust that God is directing every step you take. It is so easy to get caught up in trying to plan out and visualize where God is taking us that we can miss valuable lessons along the way and get off track. When God gives you a dream and a purpose to fulfill, it will always require faith and dependence upon Him. If your dream is small enough that you can accomplish it in your own strength and wisdom, then it's probably not the complete picture of what God wants to accomplish through your life. Just embrace the journey and take everything one day at a time. Don't allow yourself to be overwhelmed. God will make His plan known to you, if you seek and desire to know it. He will help you live it out and make it a reality. If God says it, He will do it (Isaiah 14:24) and He is not a man, that He should lie (Numbers 23:19).

Remember, God's Word does not return to Him void (Isaiah 55:11). Embrace the journey ahead, knowing that the Lord is with you and He is the one that will help His plan through your life come to pass.

VARIABLES ON THE JOURNEY

God will use willing and available people, businesses, organizations, and other means to bring you to the place where He can get the most impact out of your life. Don't worry, doubt, or become disappointed when the road isn't what you expected or how you expected. Know that your life is in God's hands and obey His Word and direction. Remain in a place of "Yes" and keep your heart pure.

God works in mysterious ways and we will not always understand, but we don't always have to. We only need to yield to Him and follow His voice. Don't miss opportunities, provision, breakthroughs, and blessing because of fear, procrastination, insecurity, unbelief, or pride. He is God and we are not. Don't be so analytical in trying to figure out what God is doing that you stress yourself out in the process. You must have confidence that if you remain in relationship with Him, He will lead you, and remaining submitted to Him ensures that you are not going to miss what He has for you.

WHO?

God loves using His family to fulfill the dreams He has for us. We should not assume that we are going to get to our destination alone. Now, I know that people can be wishy washy. There may be seasonal friendships and involvement with God's vision for your life. That is okay. God will use people that are in faith agreement as a support system and Kingdom Family unit to manifest His plan. He may even use people you would never expect. In the Word, God used Rahab, a prostitute, who had great faith and is in the lineage of Jesus (read the Book of Joshua). God can use anyone and we don't want to judge them, because they may be the person that God uses to open a door.

I will say that it is imperative that we don't become dependent on people without being aware of it. You can make idols of them if you seek them out for help and advice before you go to God. Any person you place before God is an idol. This is how people slip into manipulation and toxic motives. Let God bring people into your life. Ask Him if they are supposed to be close to you, if you can trust them. If God trusts a person, there is a measure of relational safety. Another thing to consider is that sometimes, certain people are only in your life for one season. For various reasons, God may not allow them to remain close to you as seasons change, and that is okay. Trust God to lead you in all of your friendships and relationships. There is more about this in the chapter titled "The Alignment."

HOW?

There are numerous ways that God can help you arrive to your destiny. People may fail you and challenging circumstances may happen, but God always has a way. I think of it like a maze that has thousands of ways to get from start to finish. God is so good that He will always reroute us when necessary. No matter what happens in life, He has a solution and the direction we need. God may use unexpected methods for transitioning or moving you through life to get to your destiny. The Lord used a donkey to get where He was going (Mark 11). He can use all kinds of situations, organizations, scholarships, contacts, businesses, and life experiences, etc. When one door closes, He will open another. When we fail, God never will. He is so faithful to help us get back on track when we repent and return to Him.

WHEN?

Ecclesiastes 3:1 says, "For everything there is a season, a time for every activity under heaven." Everything will happen in God's timing. God moves through seasons. Sometimes there are sovereign, God-ordained moments of opportunity and open doors. But often timing is connected with our level of readiness. Your procrastination or refusal to get inner healing and freedom in areas that you know God keeps speaking to you about can delay things. However, God is so good at redeeming time. On the other hand, moving too fast, speaking too soon, and racing ahead of God can be detrimental. Be at peace and trust that His timing is perfect. Stay sensitive to Him by staying in sync with Him through prayer. God's timing is more important to you than your time clock. Your judgment can get cloudy and you can convince yourself to move out of God's intended time frame. There will be no grace or favor on that.

You must stay sensitive to the voice of God so that you will be able to recognize key people, vehicles, times, and seasons. This requires letting "the Holy Spirit guide your lives. Then you won't be doing what your sinful nature craves" (Galatians 5:16). You never want to miss appointments with destiny, so you must be totally dependent on God and let His Word be the lamp to your feet and the light to your path (Psalm 119:105), revealing truth and bringing clarity.

DON'T RUN

Once you are aware of your purpose, don't run from the calling of God. Keep your "YES." You will find no greater joy and satisfaction in life than when you are operating in God's purpose and making a difference. Once you really have a revelation of what you were created to do, nothing else in life will fully satisfy or fulfill you more. The more you walk toward your life-purpose, the more awe, wonder, excitement, and passion will rise within you. When you realize that you have the ability to change the lives of people around you, and that you were created to live a life that's about more than yourself, what a wonderful thing that is!

Once you know your purpose, running from it is not wise. Aside from the fact that you just won't be truly happy outside of what you were born to do, life will be harder outside of the favor and blessings of God. Do not rebel after your ears have been opened (Ezekiel 12:2).

The Book of Jonah shows us an excellent example of what happens when we run from God's calling. Jonah's life purpose was to be a prophet and spokesperson for the Lord. God gave him specific instructions to go to Nineveh and speak a strong word to the people there. Nineveh was the capitol of Assyria. These were pagan, wicked people who were enemies of Israel, and their army was one of the most feared in the world. I can imagine that fear was one of the primary reasons that Jonah chose not to obey God's instruction. Instead, he ran away and got on a ship headed in the opposite direction of Nineveh. The ship encountered a huge storm that tossed it almost to the point of breaking, sinking, and killing everyone on board.

With all that was going on, Jonah was actually sleeping! The captain on the ship woke him up saying, "Call out to your God. We are all going to die!" Jonah immediately knew why they were all experiencing the storm and faced with death—it was because of his disobedience. He had them throw him overboard and the storm ceased immediately. Jonah was swallowed by a huge fish, and in the fish's belly, he repented before God. After those three days and nights in the belly of the fish and repenting, God shot Jonah out of the belly of the fish to the original destination he was called to: Nineveh. Now, of course, that's just my nutshell version of the story, but you get the point.

When you run from your life purpose, you and the people around you go through "unnecessary storms." All of us go through storms in life (tribulations, hard times, etc.), but I'm talking about unnecessary storms that could have been avoided and prevented if you were living a completely surrendered life, pursuing God's call. The longer you run from God—or don't surrender completely to Him—the more unnecessary storms you will go through. If you made the decision today to say "Yes" to God's will, to obey His Word, and to spread the Gospel in your own unique way, people around you will be blessed as a result. Hopefully, reading this book will eliminate a lot of unnecessary storms and wasted time in your life. You can say "Yes" to God's call on your life and avoid hardships that result from bad decisions and living on the run.

The belly of the fish in the story of Jonah represents a "tight place." Sometimes in life, you mess things up so badly that you have no option but to surrender or die. We must surrender our lives to God completely and stop the back-and-forth and on-the fence lifestyle. The belly of the fish experience is not fun. That's when you feel pressure on every side, like everything seems to be falling apart; then you finally realize that God is your only option. In the belly of the fish, Jonah had no choice but to cry out to God, creating the perfect opportunity for repentance. After Jonah said "Yes" to his calling and repented from running, God positioned him exactly where he needed to be to walk in the prophetic calling that was on his life. So, the good news is that if you have been running, you can repent and ask God to launch you into the place He wants you to be to get back on track. It is possible that God could make up for lost time, redeeming everything that you lost during your time of rebellion.

Personally, I know this story very well. As I previously mentioned, I became aware of my life purpose shortly after becoming a Christian. However, I played "Jonah" for years before giving God a real "Yes." It seemed that whenever I would start getting strong in my faith, teaching vacation Bible school classes and being invited to speak on a couple of occasions in church, the enemy would attack hard. He attacked me because I'm a person of purpose and he is scared of what I can accomplish for God. The enemy has so much fear and anxiety about your "Yes" and lifestyle of obedience to God.

The children of Israel were people of purpose. As children of God, through their bloodline, Jesus would be brought into this world. You and I are people of purpose, bringing Jesus into this world, as we share our faith. The enemy tries to prevent God's kingdom and will from coming to pass through us on earth as it is in heaven. I didn't know how to handle the attacks I experienced. That's the reason I've written this book: to teach others how to fight for their purpose, so they don't have to go through unnecessary storms and junk like I went through. You will learn more about how to fight in later chapters.

I didn't know how to fight through the traumatic events that hunted me down. These events were like the task masters Pharaoh assigned over the children of Israel and the army he sent after them as they were on their Exodus escape. Exodus 15:9 says,

"The enemy boasted, 'I will chase them and catch up with them. I will plunder them and consume them. I will flash my sword; my powerful hand will destroy them.'"

It was almost like "disaster" was a detective that was always looking for me, searching for me, and tracking me. I ran from my calling for much longer than I would ever recommend to anyone. I was completely oblivious as to how to deal with the continual chasing of the enemy and the unnecessary storms I placed myself in. I didn't realize that if I would have stayed committed to God in the hard times, that the Lord would have consumed my enemies and attackers as He did for the children of Israel, swallowing up their oppressors in the Red Sea (Exodus 14). In a "fight or flight" situation, learn how to fight for your purpose. The enemy was trying to kill me, steal from me, and destroy me before I could recognize who I was. He should have done that when he had the chance, because I know who I am now! Hallelujah! You don't have to be ignorant like I was; you can save time and get to the main event of your life purpose. Find out who you are in God NOW and say Yes!

SELF-WORK

Spend some time in prayer asking God to show you His specific plan for your life. Practice listening. Journal what you hear, see, and feel that God is saying to you about your purpose. Even if you are a little unsure, write it down and ask God to confirm it to you. What are you willing to do for God? If you somewhat understand your purpose already, have you been running? Ask yourself, "What have been the consequences of that?"

(Journal these things out on a separate piece of paper.)

2.5 THE SUPERNATURAL HELP_

Wouldn't it be great if the perfect person came alongside you to help with everything in life? He would lead you and guide you through important decisions and would give you strength and encouragement during difficult times. He would remind you of the truth, help you in your weaknesses, intercede for you, and help you fight through opposition. He could empower you to be the best you could possibly be! Wow... I think we all need someone like that! This Person I'm speaking about actually exists; He is the Holy Spirit. We hear about the Spirit of God and read about the Holy Ghost, but God wants us to have a personal experience and relationship with Him.

Most people have misconceptions and misunderstandings of who the Holy Spirit is until they meet Him for themselves. Christians haven't always accurately displayed or explained who He is. I apologize if He has ever been misrepresented to you. Let me introduce you to my best friend who has been my supernatural help: the Holy Spirit.

HELLO, HOLY SPIRIT

Unbelievers are blinded to the truth (2 Corinthians 4:4). The

Bible explains in 1 Corinthians 2:14, "But people who aren't spiritual can't receive these truths from God's Spirit. It all sounds foolish to them and they can't understand it, for only those who are spiritual can understand what the Spirit means."

Our first introduction to the Holy Spirit comes when we become believers. It is by the Holy Spirit that we receive the revelation of who Jesus is and become Christians. The Holy Spirit brings the supernatural revelation of Truth for salvation (1 Corinthians 12:3) so people are clearly able to feel and know that Jesus is Lord and God is real. Something spiritual takes place when someone gives their life to God and starts his or her faith journey. The Holy Spirit is working inside us at the salvation moment. And at that moment, we become a son or daughter of God because a spiritual adoption takes place through the Holy Spirit (Romans 8:14-17) and God becomes our Father.

Ephesians 3:17 says, "Then Christ will make his home in your hearts as you trust in him. Your roots will grow down into God's love and keep you strong."

How does Jesus actually make His home in your heart? Through the Holy Spirit at salvation. There is a second work of the Holy Spirit that is available to us. Jesus talked to the disciples about a monumental moment that was to come. He said they were to wait in Jerusalem until they experienced the infilling of the Baptism of the Holy Spirit.

Luke 24:49 says, "And now I will send the Holy Spirit, just as my Father promised. But stay here in the city until the Holy Spirit comes and fills you with power from heaven."

You can absolutely choose to live your life without the filling of power from heaven, but why would you want to? In fact, Ephesians 5:18 commands that we be filled with the Fruit of the Holy Spirit every day.

Acts 1:8 tells us, "But you shall receive power (ability, efficiency, and might) when the Holy Spirit has come upon you, and you shall be my witnesses in Jerusalem and all Judea and Samaria and to the ends (the very bounds) of the earth" (AMP).

The primary purpose of having Holy Spirit's power is to be a witness. This means that in everything you do, His power dwells within you to prove to the world that God is love and to demonstrate to the world that He is real. With the supernatural guidance and direction of the Holy Spirit, it's like having navigation for your calling and God-purpose in life. This is not only desirable for you, but for those who are lost who are watching your life. As the power of God operates in you through His Spirit, everything in life is easier. His way is always better than ours. His Spirit allows us to be better connected with His plan and will for us as individuals.

LIMITLESS JESUS

Jesus makes a shocking statement in John 16:7. He said, "However, I am telling you nothing but the truth when I say it is profitable (good, expedient, advantageous) for you that I go away. Because if I do not go away, the Comforter (Counselor, Helper, Advocate, Intercessor, Strengthener, Standby) will not come to you [into close fellowship with you]; but if I go away, I will send Him to you [to be in close fellowship with you]" (AMP).

In our natural understanding, it would seem better to have Jesus personally with you in physical form, but here He says it's an advantage and better for you to have the Holy Spirit. After Jesus died on the cross, He rose from the dead, spent some time with the disciples, ascended into heaven, and He is now at the right hand of Father God making intercession for us (Romans 8:34). The Holy Spirit, the Spirit that was upon Jesus, descended to earth on Pentecost to fill believers so that the Kingdom of God could be multiplied through yielded vessels doing the work of the Lord Jesus. So, this is how God the Father (on the throne), Jesus the Son (on the right hand of the Father interceding for us), and the Holy Spirit (now on the earth, filling believers) can all be separate Entities, but One. This is how Jesus is the Lord God wrapped in flesh, filled with the Spirit of God. His virgin mother Mary was impregnated by the Holy Spirit to give birth to Him (Matthew 1:18), making Jesus fully human and fully God at the same time. Jesus, the Word of God, walked this earth in physical form and was anointed with the Spirit of God. This is a quick explanation, but if you're confused about all this, I encourage you to do a Bible study on the topic of the Trinity.

Jesus wants you to receive the Baptism of the Holy Spirit, be filled with power from heaven, and be everything that God created you to be as His child. Ephesians 1:23 explains, "And the church is his body; it is made full and complete by Christ, who fills all things everywhere with himself."

Jesus wants to fill us with Himself. Divine union, being mingled into Him as one. The Holy Spirit is actually the same Spirit that was within and upon Jesus. As the Son of God, He was restricted when He walked the earth in the physical form of a human being. He could only minister to people, heal people, perform miracles for people in the geographic area He was in. This is why He said "it's better for Me to go away, die on the cross, raise from the dead, and take my place at the right hand of the Father," so that the Holy Spirit can come and fill people as we just saw in the book of Acts.

Ephesians 4:9-10 says, "Notice that it says 'he ascended.' This clearly means that Christ also descended to our lowly world. And the same one who descended is the one who ascended higher than all the heavens, so that he might fill the entire universe with himself."

He fills us with Himself. Now we are able to carry the same Holy Spirit that operated through Jesus. The Spirit of Jesus, the Holy Spirit, is now unlimited on the earth and moves across the globe so that through us, the Kingdom and will of God can come to earth as it is in heaven. So, our physical bodies now become the temples, dwelling places, and vehicles that God uses to bring Jesus to the world. God chose to work through the person of Jesus, and now because of what Jesus did on the cross, He continues to work through people to accomplish His plan. We have become His children through what His Son did for us and we are sealed by the Holy Spirit, the same Spirit that was in and upon Jesus, the same powerful Holy Spirit that raised Jesus from the dead. Don't you want more of Him? If you want more of Jesus, you want more of the Holy Spirit!

Romans 8:11 says, "The Spirit of God, who raised Jesus from the dead, lives in you. And just as God raised Christ Jesus from the dead, he will give life to your mortal bodies by this same Spirit living within you."

SUPERNATURAL HELP MAKES US DIFFERENT

There is a difference between a person who deals with obstacles in life with power and those who grapple with circumstances powerless. Everywhere the disciples went after they were filled with God's power, they asked people if they had been filled and baptized with the Holy Spirit. Acts 8:15 explains, "As soon as they arrived, they prayed for these new believers to receive the Holy Spirit." It doesn't matter what your background is—Pentecostal, Methodist, Baptist, Catholic, Jewish, COGIC, or Assemblies of God—the question is, "Have you received the Holy Spirit since you first believed?" This is the same question that I ask you today.

Acts 19:1-6 reads, "While Apollos was in Corinth, Paul traveled through the interior regions until he reached Ephesus, on the coast, where he found several believers. 'Did you receive the Holy Spirit when you believed?' he asked them. 'No,' they replied, 'we haven't even heard that there is a Holy Spirit.' 'Then what baptism did you experience?' he asked. And they replied, 'The baptism of John.' Paul said, 'John's baptism called for repentance from sin. But John himself told the people to believe in the one who would come later, meaning Jesus.' As soon as they heard this, they were baptized in the name of the Lord Jesus. Then when Paul laid his hands on them, the Holy Spirit came on them, and they spoke in other tongues and prophesied."

The infilling of the Spirit in a person's life is only the beginning. It's not just about the "feel good" experience and the power, but about a relationship. Unfortunately, believers miss out on getting to know the Person of the Holy Spirit intimately. I was saved for many years before I realized that I didn't know the Holy Spirit as well as I thought I did. It's like living in the same house with someone and only talking to that other person when you need to. You hear them, feel their movement, see them every once in a while, but you don't really spend much time just sitting with them, talking and listening, and getting to know them more. Your body is the temple (house) of the Holy Spirit (1 Corinthians 6:19-20); would you ever want to have a tenant in your house that you didn't really know? Some people are okay with not knowing Him, if He pays rent on time and delivers when they need Him; that's superficial. There is so much more to the Holy Spirit than we are aware of. You can spend forever getting to know the splendor of the Holy Spirit more and more.

THE HOLY SPIRIT'S WORK DEFINED

The Holy Spirit:

- Empowers you (Acts 1:8)
- Gives you life (John 6:63)
- Is your Counselor and Helper (John 14:26)
- Is your Comforter (John 14:16; John 14:26; John 15:26)
- Is your Teacher (John 14:26)
- Is the power of the resurrection (Romans 8:11)
- Testifies of Jesus (John 15:26)

- Gives supernatural gifts to you (1 Corinthians 12:8-10; Romans 12:6-7)
- Strengthens and encourages you (Acts 9:31)
- Leads and guides you (Romans 8:14)
- Reveals truth to you (John 16:13)
- Helps you in your weaknesses (Romans 8:26)
- Intercedes for you (Romans 8:26)
- Searches the deep things of God (1 Corinthians 2:10)
- Sanctifies you (1 Corinthians 6:11)
- Reminds you of the Word (John 14:26)
- Edifies you (1 Corinthians 14:4)
- Builds you up (Jude 1:20)
- Gives you rest (Isaiah 28)
- Refreshes you (Acts 3:19-21)
- Convicts and forbids you (John 16:8; Acts 16:6-7)
- Brings love, joy, peace, patience, kindness, goodness, faithfulness, gentleness, and self-control to you (Galatians 5:22-23)
- Hovered the waters of the earth during creation (Genesis 1:1-2)
- Took part in the conception of Jesus within a virgin (Matthew 1:18)
- Was present during the baptism of Jesus (Matthew 3:16)
- Was present during the resurrection of Jesus (Romans 8:11)

HOW TO RECEIVE HOLY SPIRIT

You may be thinking, "All of this sounds great, but I've never experienced being filled with the Holy Spirit." Salvation is a prerequisite. The Bible says in Romans 10:9-10, "If you confess with your mouth that Jesus is Lord and believe in your heart that God raised him from the dead, you will be saved. For it is by believing in your heart that you are made right with God, and it is by confessing with your mouth that you are saved."

The next step is to simply ask. We already know it is God's plan and will for your life to be filled with the power of the Holy Spirit. Believe that God wants it for you even more than you want it for yourself!

In Luke 11:11-13, Jesus asked, "You fathers—if your children ask for a fish, do you give them a snake instead? Or if they ask for an egg, do you give them a scorpion? Of course not! So if you sinful people know how to give good gifts to your children, how much more will your heavenly Father give the Holy Spirit to those who ask him."

Don't get discouraged if it doesn't happen right away. Continue to ask. There are a few things that generally hinder people from being baptized in the Holy Spirit: fear, pride, confusion, overthinking, and feelings of unworthiness. Pray that God removes these things from your life. Ask for other Spirit-filled believers to pray for you while laying hands so that you may be filled (Acts 8:17).

HOW DOES HOLY SPIRIT MOVE?

There are several ways that Holy Spirit shows up or manifests. He comes like fire, wind, warmth, peace, a river, a whirlwind, a tidal wave, chills, joy, drunken laughter, and more. I love the way He moves, however He wants to move. For the sake of the specifics of being filled with Holy Spirit and thirsting for more of Him, let's discuss the prophetic symbolism of water.

"On the last day, the climax of the festival, Jesus stood and shouted to the crowds, 'Anyone who is thirsty may come to me! Anyone who believes in me may come and drink! For the Scriptures declare, Rivers of living water will flow from his heart.' When he said 'living water,' he was speaking of the Spirit, who would be given to everyone believing in him. But the Spirit had not yet been given, because Jesus had not yet entered into his glory" (John 7:37-39).

Now that you know a little bit more about who the Holy Spirit is, I'm going to talk to you about how the Spirit of God flows. The Word refers to the Spirit of God like a river of water. He is like a supernatural river flowing from the throne of God. This can't be seen with the natural eyes, but it can be felt. The book of Daniel refers to it as a fiery stream (Daniel 7:10). God doesn't want you to just have a sip of Him, but to depend on consistently drinking from the River, continually being refreshed and filled with Him.

Revelation 22:1-2 says, "Then the angel showed me a river with the water of life, clear as crystal, flowing from the throne of God and of the Lamb. It flowed down the center of the main street. On each side of the river grew a tree of life, bearing twelve crops of fruit, with a fresh crop each month. The leaves were used for medicine to heal the nations."

We should desire the Spirit of God just like the deer that pants for the water brooks. You drink, find refreshment, satisfy your thirst, wash in the water to be cleansed and to remove the residue from your past. "As the deer longs for streams of water, so I long for you, O God. I thirst for God, the living God..." (Psalm 42:1-2).

There is nothing more refreshing than spending time with God. He washes away every worry, concern, fear, sin, and frustration and helps you get out of your flesh, out of your own way. You find healing and freedom when you tap into the flowing river of God's Spirit.

The Lord spoke through the prophet Elisha and told Namaan to dip seven times in the river. It took seven times for him to be healed of his leprosy. See, you come to church on Sunday, dip once, and expect everything to be fine, but you can't live life hoping that a spiritual experience you had a while ago will be enough to help you through the rest of life. It's about a relationship with the Holy Spirit in which you continually dip in the flowing river and are filled. Don't allow yourself to get stale; you are not supposed to be an isolated pond, but connected to the river of His Spirit.

Hopefully, at the conclusion of this chapter, you see the importance of being filled with the Holy Spirit and have a desire to discover more of who He is. The more you know the Spirit of God, the more you will know Jesus and the more you will know yourself. There are so many benefits that come from having a relationship with the Spirit of God. You will continue to mature and go deeper in your ability to understand and comprehend the Holy Spirit. As you grow, God will use you more and more to do great things on the earth for Him with the empowerment of the Holy Ghost! The characteristics and gifts of the Holy Spirit are amazing!

SELF-WORK

Below are attributes of the Holy Spirit. Put a check next to the ones that you personally know and continually experience in your life and relationship with the Person of the Holy Spirit. Any characteristics that remain blank are areas that I encourage you to pursue knowing Him.

- Counselor and Helper (John 14:26)
- Comforter (John 14:16; John 14:26; John 15:26)
- Teacher (John 14:26)
- Resurrection power (Romans 8:11)
- Testifies of Jesus (John 15:26)
- Gives supernatural gifts (1 Corinthians 12:8-10; Romans 12:6-7)
- Strengthens and encourages (Acts 9:31)
- Leads (Romans 8:14)
- Reveals truth (John 16:13)

- Helps us in our weaknesses (Romans 8:26)
- Intercedes (Romans 8:26)
- Searches the deep things of God (1 Corinthians 2:10)
- Sanctifies (1 Corinthians 6:11)
- Reminds us of the Word (John 14:26)
- Edifies you (1 Corinthians 14:4)
- Builds you up (Jude 1:20)
- Gives you rest (Isaiah 28)
- Refreshes you (Acts 3:19-21)
- Convicts and forbids (John 16:8; Acts 16:6-7)
- Love (Galatians 5:22-23)
- Joy (Galatians 5:22-23)
- Peace (Galatians 5:22-23)
- Patience (Galatians 5:22-23)
- Kindness (Galatians 5:22-23)
- Goodness (Galatians 5:22-23)
- Faithfulness (Galatians 5:22-23)
- Gentleness (Galatians 5:22-23)
- Self-Control (Galatians 5:22-23)

2.6 THE GIFTS_

This is where it gets fun! There are major benefits of having the Holy Spirit living in your life, other than the exciting relationship with Jesus that He magnifies. Holy Spirit empowers us with supernatural character-building fruit, gifts, talents, and abilities. It's like having our very own superpowers to serve humanity and advance the Kingdom of God! There are college courses and several books written on this topic, so I am just going to give you an extremely simplified explanation of these gifts; I do not proclaim to be an expert in the area of supernatural gifts. However, learning about the gifts God placed in my life helped me discover and live out my purpose, which was a huge milestone in my personal life journey. I have seen more of God's value and self-worth within me as I have been used by Him to accomplish assignments. It is very rewarding to be used by the Holy Spirit to draw people to the Lord. Supernatural gifts operating in your life can cause the unbeliever to believe. Often, I have the privilege of introducing someone to Jesus because of a gift of the Holy Spirit operating.

It is important to discover the gifts that are in you through the Holy Spirit in order to steward them well and grow in wisdom for their use. You must realize that the gifts are never about you, but about God drawing people to Him as well as drawing believers even closer to Him. The gifts of the Holy Spirit are about God's Kingdom coming and His Will being done on the earth as it is in heaven. The gifts are about God manifesting Himself to reveal who He really is and fulfilling what His Word says.

There are three general classifications of spiritual gifts: Gifts of the Spirit, Functional Gifts, and Ascension Gifts (Fivefold Ministry Gifts). Pause—I must make a very clear point before getting into the descriptions of spiritual gifts. Without LOVE, your gifts and talents are useless. I have seen many gifted people who did not walk in love while trying to function in a spiritual gift and it did more damage than good. The enemy knows this and will always try to tempt gifted people to operate outside the anointed boundaries of LOVE. If he can get your focus off love, then you won't be as effective in using the gifts God has placed in you. The enemy frequently and strategically tempts and attacks gifted people with three things to strip them of the flow of God's powerful love.

1. PRIDE

In the area of supernatural gifts, pride is seen in the temptation to take credit for what God has done. It is taking God's glory and pointing to yourself, your own flesh, human strength, or what "you" did. It is bowing to your need for applause or acknowledgement, when God is supposed to get all of the glory. The enemy doesn't want God to be glorified. Remember, pride stopped Satan from being used in his original gifting (Revelation 12:7-12). LOVE is not boastful or proud (1 Corinthians 13:4-5)! When miracles happen through you, it is by the Holy Spirit through you and the power of Jesus. Keep that in perspective even when people try to praise or flatter you.

2. ACCUSATION

Accusations of others take place when we yield to the temptation to be judgmental and communicate shame, guilt, and condemnation because of what you see or know about people. People who have strong discernment or words of knowledge are very tempted by judgment and accusation. This includes gossiping about private matters and intentionally exposing people's sins or issues and to have the mentality of being better than or more spiritual than others. Remember, when you get insight on sin or the demonic happening in the life of another, it is to pray for them or release freedom to them as Holy Spirit leads. You are not given information to just talk about people or make them feel bad. Pull them up higher to the greater reality of the Kingdom. Your love and kindness will help lead them to repentance (Romans 2:4). The enemy doesn't want people to be forgiven, free, and transformed to be like Christ. Accusation can even work against you in forms such as insecurity, low self-esteem, low self-worth, depression, or constantly being "past focused." The enemy is the accuser of God's children (Revelation 12:10), but LOVE covers a multitude of sins (1 Peter 4:8)!

3. FEAR

The enemy tries to back you down and shut you up by scaring and intimidating you. He tries to rob you of your authority in Christ because he is shaking in his boots, afraid of what God can do through you. He has no power over you at all unless you give it to him, but you'll learn more about that in a later chapter. God has not given you a spirit of fear, but the Spirit of power, love, and a sound mind (2 Timothy 1:7). You don't want to minister to people out of fear. This can quickly turn into trying to control, manipulate, or influence from a religious spirit. His perfect LOVE casts out, drives out, and expels fear (1 John 4:18). If God reveals something to you, it is because it is on His heart to do something about it. There is no pressure on you to perform or make something happen. Operate in faith, NOT fear.

First Corinthians 13:1-3 says, "If I could speak all the languages of earth and of angels, but didn't love others, I would only be a noisy gong or a clanging cymbal. If I had the gift of prophecy, and if I understood all of God's secret plans and possessed all knowledge, and if I had such faith that I could move mountains, but didn't love others, I would be nothing. If I gave everything I have to the poor and even sacrificed my body, I could boast about it; but if I didn't love others, I would have gained nothing." If people feel more separated from God as a result of the gifts we are functioning in, then we need to get some healing and freedom, because we have missed it entirely. Okay, now let's proceed with understanding the gifts!

THE GIFTS OF THE SPIRIT

The gifts of the Spirit move as the Holy Spirit wills. They are for the edification of the body of Christ and a sign to the unbeliever that God is real. These gifts can operate one-on- one, in a group, or in a corporate setting. The focus must always be on God; the gifts of the Spirit never detract from what He is doing. With lack of understanding, these gifts can be misused, demonstrated completely out of order, out of God's timing, and even in the flesh if human desires are mixed with the moving of the Holy Spirit.

The enemy tries to mimic these gifts sometimes, as well. So please don't ignore this section if you've seen some crazy hocus-pocus person acting weird or if someone has ever lied to you, saying they were prophesying for the Lord. Don't intentionally cut off part of who God is because of the way you've seen another person act. The gifts of God are not what everyone has illustrated them to be, so you should learn about them for yourself. Ask God to open up your understanding of the gifts. Forgive and release anyone who has "ministered" to you improperly, claiming to be flowing in the gifts of God. Don't let the false things people have done in the past pervert the truth about the fullness of God for you. The gifts of the Spirit are very real and God wants to stir them up and use them in you. It is imperative that you are sensitive to the timing and the way in which God will use the gifts of the Spirit in your life. You can be used as a beautiful instrument of the Lord to bring about His will.

First Corinthians 12:4-11 explains, "There are different kinds of spiritual gifts, but the same Spirit is the source of them all. There are different kinds of service, but we serve the same Lord. God works in different ways, but it is the same God who does the work in all of us. A spiritual gift is given to each of us so we can help each other. To one person the Spirit gives the ability to give wise advice; to another the same Spirit gives a message of special knowledge. The same Spirit gives great faith to another, and to someone else the one Spirit gives the gift of healing. He gives one person the power to perform miracles, and another the ability to prophesy. He gives someone else the ability to discern whether a message is from the Spirit of God or from another spirit. Still another person is given the ability to speak in unknown languages, while another is given the ability to interpret what is being said. It is the one and only Spirit who distributes all these gifts. He alone decides which gift each person should have."

THE WORD OF WISDOM

The word of wisdom is defined as the supernatural ability to know how to apply the Word and Truth, resulting in divine instruction and guidance. Wisdom gives the blueprint and the "how to" accomplish what God wants to do. This gift is sometimes partnered with the gift of the word of knowledge and/or prophecy.

THE WORD OF KNOWLEDGE

The word of knowledge is the supernatural ability to know things in the present or the past. This information is only given by the Holy Spirit and there is no other way that you could arrive at the same conclusion using your own natural assumptions. This is how you can know exactly what's going on in someone's life without them telling you anything. This gift partners with several others, particularly the gift of healing, and comes to the forefront during intercessory prayer, as well. The word of knowledge brings a divine supernatural "knowing." Many times, I've felt a very specific thing in my body as a "word of knowledge," then when I release the things God wants to heal in the room, the individuals dealing with that specific thing receive healing through Jesus.

THE GIFT OF FAITH

The gift of faith is the supernatural ability to consistently believe God for what appears to be impossible in the natural. It is the faith to see God do what cannot be done naturally. This gift is usually partnered with the gifts of healing and the working of miracles. We sometimes call this gift "Crazy Faith"!

THE WORD OF HEALING

The gift of healing brings the consistent supernatural ability to lay hands on the sick so that they recover. People moving in these gifts may speak a word of knowledge and see God heal. They might also simply pray for someone in person (or not in person) and healing is manifested. Consistently, healing miracles happen around the person who has this gift.

THE WORKING OF MIRACLES

When the Holy Spirit is working miracles, His supernatural ability changes the way the universe naturally operates. This causes something that occurs naturally to shift or change in a way that could only be done by the Spirit of God. Some examples in the Bible are the parting the Red Sea, causing the sun to stand still in the Book of Joshua, Jesus walking on the water, or causing an arm or leg to grow that was missing from birth. Signs and wonders are miracles that follow those who believe.

THE GIFT OF PROPHECY

When someone is being used by God in the gift of prophecy, the Holy Spirit gives him or her the supernatural ability to see what is happening in the supernatural realm and revealing the future. To prophesy is to sense and know God's intended plan that is yet to be fulfilled and sometimes to speak it into existence. To prophesy is also to feel God's heart and speak out His words as His mouthpiece. When someone is prophesied over in public, it is like God's public display of affection. The fulfillment of some prophecies is conditional, and is based upon the faith actions of the recipient of that prophetic word. However, some prophecies are sovereign and come to pass no matter what. There are so many components of this gifting; it makes for a great Bible study.

THE DISCERNING OF SPIRITS

This gift of the Spirit is the supernatural ability to know whether a spirit is of God or not of God. Those used in this gift are able to identify specific spirits, rulers, authorities, wickedness in high places, and workers of the enemy. This gift can be manifested through seeing, feeling, knowing, or hearing. This gift also opens spiritual eyes to see angelic activity. The spirit realm appears to be more vivid, through all the senses, than the natural ream with this gift.

THE GIFT OF SPEAKING IN TONGUES

This gift gives a believer the supernatural ability to speak in another language that they have never learned. It can be used to communicate a message from God for the edification of the Body of Christ (Acts 2:6).

THE GIFT OF INTERPRETING MESSAGES IN TONGUES

This is the supernatural ability to interpret a message given in tongues, a message in a language that you've never learned, the ability to convey what God is saying to other believers for their edification. I have a missionary friend who was given the interpretation of the Portuguese language through an encounter with God in the night. The Lord was arranging to marry her to a pastor from Brazil. What a miraculous gift and a conformation to their heavenly union for the Glory of God in Brazil!

THE FUNCTIONAL OR MOTIVATIONAL GIFTS

These gifts function in a person's life on a consistent basis. They are talented and spiritually gifted in these areas and are continually tapping into the motivational gifts God has given to them. These motivational gifts are part of who they are and are often thought of as part of their personality. They frequently demonstrate their motivational gifts in daily life.

In Romans 12:6-8, 13, the Bible says, "In his grace, God has given us different gifts for doing certain things well. So, if God has given you the ability to prophesy, speak out with as much faith as God has given you. If your gift is serving others, serve them well. If you are a teacher, teach well. If your gift is to encourage others, be encouraging. If it is giving, give generously. If God has given you leadership ability, take the responsibility seriously. And if you have a gift for showing kindness to others, do it gladly... distributing to the needs of the saints, given to hospitality."

THE GIFT OF PROPHECY

This is the same gift that appears in the list of spiritual gifts in 1 Corinthians 12:4-11. It is the supernatural ability to see and proclaim either what is currently happening in the supernatural realm or revealing the future.

THE GIFT OF SERVING (MINISTRY)

This gift gives believers the supernatural ability to recognize needs and effectively respond with compassion, love, and excellence. A person with this gift loves working hard for the Kingdom of God, no matter what that entails. He or she looks forward to opportunities to serve and finds fulfillment in life through serving because it gives them great joy. They are not complainers and don't mind "busting a sweat" for Jesus.

THE GIFT OF TEACHING

The gift of teaching is the supernatural ability to explain the Word of God with simplicity and in a way that anyone could learn and be enlightened with truth. The people with this gift have a strong hunger and love for God's Word. They are teachers by nature and actually can teach anything!

THE GIFT OF ENCOURAGEMENT OR EXHORTATION

This is the supernatural ability to inspire and motivate people. It is an ability to see and develop potential in people's lives. A person with this gift encourages others to see things from God's point of view and look at the positive side of situations. This gift brings a spiritual uplift to people so that they actually feel better after being in the presence of a person with this gift.

THE GIFT OF GIVING

This gift brings the supernatural ability to produce an income for the purpose of supporting the ministry, pouring out provision that far surpasses regular tithes and offerings. It makes those operating in this gift able to give with simplicity and without expecting anything in return from those they help financially. Those with this gift are also able to recognize financial needs and respond to them. These people feel the joy of the Lord, godly satisfaction, and fulfillment of their life purpose in giving consistently; it's who they are. It is their ministry to see a need or a problem and be used by God to solve it financially. Since they hear the Lord's specific direction and wisdom concerning giving, they are faithful financial stewards. The treasuries of Heaven are open to them because they are trusted by God.

THE GIFT OF LEADERSHIP OR MANAGEMENT

This gift is seen in the supernatural ability to clearly cast vision and influence people to follow. They can communicate God's instructions that will accomplish God's direction. There are faithful and trustworthy to steward people and tasks for the Lord. Those with this gift will create a plan when there is no plan because of the gifted ability to lead that God has placed in them.

THE GIFT OF KINDNESS OR MERCY

This gift can be understood as a supernatural sensitivity to the issues, hurts, and concerns of others. It is also seen as a nonjudgmental desire to help people through their hard times and love them through their difficulties and shortcomings. It's characterized by empathy and a strong spiritual desire to minister to the hurting, no matter how deep and dark their world may be. Those with this gift are kind, sweet, patient, understanding, and approachable.

THE GIFT OF HOSPITALITY

This gift imparts a supernatural ability that makes people feel welcome and valuable. Those operating in this gift are able to reach and serve people in special ways that bring honor to God. They assist in creating an atmosphere of excellence that makes people feel at home and important. They are anointed faithful stewards over the materials and resources given to them or to be used by them. Even when they are not serving in the role of hospitality, they are nice, friendly people that make others feel welcome.

First Corinthians 12:28 has another list of spiritual gifts; it says, "And God has appointed these in the church: first apostles, second prophets, third teachers, after that miracles, then gifts of healings, helps, administrations, varieties of tongues."

THE GIFT OF HELPS

The gift of helps can be explained as a supernatural desire to help leaders, pastors, and ministries accomplish God's purpose with excellence. It is sometimes seen as a "go-getter" or hard-worker mentality and is marked by the spiritual strength, endurance, and joy in serving. "How can I help?" is a frequent question from a person who has this functional gift. Some examples are: armor bearers, health care workers, service industry, or assistants to a leader.

THE GIFT OF ADMINISTRATION OR GOVERNMENTS

This gift is seen as both a supernatural ability and a desire to create strategy and organize details to bring a vision to fruition. This gift displays a special spiritual wisdom and authority to delegate people and inspire involvement to fulfill the big picture. Those operating in this gift are great with time management and are known to be finishers of tasks they set out to do.

THE ASCENSION GIFTS OR FIVEFOLD MINISTRY MANTLES

When Jesus ascended to His Father, He gave gifts to men. Jesus was an Apostle, a Prophet, an Evangelist, a Pastor, and a Teacher, fulfilling all five ministries of the Fivefold Ministry. When He ascended, by His grace, He gave His supernatural mantles to men to continue His work on the earth. Through the Holy Spirit, His ministry became limitless, as explained in the previous chapter. The Holy Spirit was distributed to us. The Ascension Gifts are not just spiritual gifts that operate in a person, but they are offices that individuals walk and operate in. The people who have an Ascension Gift calling dedicate themselves to the ministry of perfecting the saints: mending, establishing, restoring, and building them up. They live to prepare, train, and equip God's people. Most importantly, they should be Christlike in the very nature of how they function in ministry. The mantle they carry is very much IDENTITY.

In Ephesians 4:7-8, 11-12 (AMP), the Bible says, "Yet grace (God's unmerited favor) was given to each of us individually [not indiscriminately, but in different ways] in proportion to the measure of Christ's [rich and bounteous] gift. Therefore it is said, When He ascended on high, He led captivity captive [He led a train of vanquished foes] and He bestowed gifts on men... And His gifts were [varied; He Himself appointed and gave men to us] some to be apostles (special messengers), some prophets (inspired preachers and expounders), some evangelists (preachers of the Gospel, traveling missionaries), some pastors (shepherds of His flock) and teachers. His intention was the perfecting and the full equipping of the saints (His consecrated people), [that they should do] the work of ministering toward building up Christ's body (the church)."

THE APOSTLE

This is the Christlike supernatural life calling to establish churches, birth ministries, bring order, and unlock spiritual gifts within people. An apostle is someone who is commissioned and sent from God as an ambassador of Jesus. They are very much like a Mama or a Papa in the Body of Christ. It is their joy to develop, encourage, and support leaders. Apostles are God's special messengers. Signs, wonders, and miracles are seen through their ministry.

THE PROPHET

The prophet has a Christlike supernatural life calling to be a spokesperson for God. Prophets foresee global, national, and local events and prophesy to every area of society. They sense what is in the heart of God and hear His voice with precision in prayer, dreams, or visions. Prophets or prophetesses have the ability to see into the spirit realm and are inspired by God to deliver messages, warnings, encouragements, and instruction. They continually edify, encourage, and build people up.

THE EVANGELIST

The evangelist has a Christlike supernatural life calling to proclaim and spread the Good News. Evangelists live to reach unbelievers with the Good News and signs and wonders usually follow their ministries. They have a supernatural boldness to speak powerful truth and will go anywhere that God sends them in order to fulfill His will. People usually gravitate toward them as they are "people persons" who enjoy connecting with absolute strangers with the motive of sharing Jesus. They are anointed soul winners; many missionaries are evangelists.

THE PASTOR

Pastors haves the Christlike supernatural life calling to be a "watchman." Pastors live to shepherd; they are continually growing a group of people. They have a strong spiritual desire to serve, protect, feed, and guide God's people. They have above average endurance and patience, as well as wisdom; they love the members of their congregations as sons and daughters. They are to provide a safe and healthy place for people to come into the family of God and grow in faith.

THE TEACHER

The teacher mantle is a Christlike supernatural life calling to instruct and enlighten people with the Truth. It is sometimes difficult to differentiate between the functional gift of teaching and the ascension gift of teacher, except that the fivefold ministry gift displays a teaching anointing to a much greater degree.

First Peter 4:10-11 says that, "God has given each of you a gift from his great variety of spiritual gifts. Use them well to serve one another. Do you have the gift of speaking? Then speak as though God himself were speaking through you. Do you have the gift of helping others? Do it with all the strength and energy that God supplies. Then everything you do will bring glory to God through Jesus Christ. All glory and power to him forever and ever! Amen."

SELF-WORK

Spend some time praying and asking God to reveal to you the spiritual gifts He has placed within you; this will likely be a progressive process. You may discover some gifts now and some others later in life. It is important to understand and know what God has placed in you so that you can grow in your knowledge and understanding of how to be used by Him more effectively. Place a checkmark next to the spiritual gifts that you feel God has given you. I encourage you to do some deeper research on the gifts, because I've shared with you a very simple surface-level teaching about them. There is so much more to each of the gifts that I do not have room to share in this book. Please search the Scriptures for yourself and ask the Holy Spirit to give you understanding and revelation.

- Word of Wisdom (1 Corinthians 12:8-10)
- Word of Knowledge (1 Corinthians 12:8-10)
- Faith (1 Corinthians 12:8-10)
- Gifts of Healing (1 Corinthians 12:8-10)
- Working of Miracles (1 Corinthians 12:8-10)
- Prophecy (1 Corinthians 12:8-10)
- Discerning of Spirits (1 Corinthians 12:8-10)
- Different Kinds of Tongues (1 Corinthians 12:8-10)
- Interpretation of Different Kinds of Tongues (1 Corinthians 12:8-10)
- Gift of Serving/Ministry (Romans 12:6-8)
- Gift of Teaching (Romans 12:6-8)
- Gift of Encouragement/Exhortation (Romans 12:6-8)
- Gift of Giving (Romans 12:6-8)
- Gift of Hospitality (Romans 12:13)
- Gift of Leadership/Management (Romans 12:6-8)
- Helps (1 Corinthians 12:28)
- Administrations/Governments (1 Corinthians 12:28)

- Gift of Kindness/Mercy (Romans 12:6-8)
- Apostle (Ephesians 4:7-8)
- Prophet (Ephesians 4:7-8)
- Evangelist (Ephesians 4:7-8)
- Pastor (Ephesians 4:7-8)
- Teacher (Ephesians 4:7-8)

2.7 THE DELAY_

There are several variables that can delay the timing of fulfilling God's purpose for our lives. Yes, God has His timing, but sometimes because of our disobedience, lack of focus, self-made limitations, bad decisions, and stinking thinking, we prolong the time that it takes to arrive at your place of purpose. If you haven't figured it out by now, let me tell you that you have a very specific God-purpose and the goal is to live out that purpose as soon as possible so that God can get the most impact out of your life.

The children of Israel spent 40 years in the wilderness (Joshua 5:6). Jesus only spent 40 days in the wilderness (Matthew 4:1). These are two examples of our transformation process, because the wilderness represents the "in-between" place. Passing through and out of the wilderness is a picture of being delivered or released out of the past while focusing on a God-purpose to live out in the future. The wilderness is designed to be temporary, not a place to live in. It is the place of dying to the flesh, maturing, growing, and denying yourself that you may receive more of God and move on to inherit the promises and destiny for your life.

This is the place of "pruning" (John 15:1-8). Jesus is the Vine and we are the branches. In the wilderness, God cuts off everything that does not bear fruit or produce good results in your life. Sometimes it hurts to have doors slammed in your face and to have friends and relationships that you didn't realize were unhealthy cut out of your life. However, it's better to embrace the process than to fight it and delay the wonderful things God has planned for you long ago. God's way is always better than our way, even when it doesn't appear to be so. You can't live up to your full potential if you cling to the very things that are stunting your growth. Welcome your life transformation, don't rebel against it.

Hebrews 3:8 admonishes, "Don't harden your hearts as Israel did when they rebelled, when they tested me in the wilderness." The length of your wilderness experience is completely up to you. You can move through it or be halted by it. For the children of Israel, it was 40 years and most of them died in the wilderness. For Jesus, it was 40 days, because He was a perfectly surrendered vessel, passed all of the tests, and overcame the trials and temptations. If you catch this revelation, what would have taken you 40 years can supernaturally take 40 days!

First Corinthians 10:1-5, 8 remind us, "I don't want you to forget, dear brothers and sisters, about our ancestors in the wilderness long ago. All of them were guided by a cloud that moved ahead of them, and all of them walked through the sea on dry ground. In the cloud and in the sea, all of them were baptized as followers of Moses. All of them ate the same spiritual food, and all of them drank the same spiritual water. For they drank from the spiritual rock that traveled with them, and that rock was Christ. Yet God was not pleased with most of them, and their bodies were scattered in the wilderness... And we must not engage in sexual immorality as some of them did, causing 23,000 of them to die in one day."

Unfortunately, many gifted, anointed, dream-filled people will die having never accomplished the very reason they were born. Not everyone is willing to make the sacrifice of living completely for Jesus. I never want to die without fulfilling my God-purpose. I chose to break out of my cycle of dependence on self, and cross over into the life God promised. The good news is that we just have to take things one day at a time and God will lead us every step of the way. God calls us, the Word renews us, and the Holy Spirit leads and guides us into all Truth.

DISTRACTIONS

It is the enemy's goal to keep Christians distracted and focused on the cares of this world instead of on their calling. He will do anything to get your mind off God's plan for your life. In fact, I will go as far to say that every single time the enemy has ever attacked you was specifically for this reason: to distract you so that God's Kingdom and will can't come to earth through you. No matter how big the attack, no matter how small, the tactics of the enemy are to kill, steal, and destroy the plan and will of God. The devil knows that God performs His will through His children. I think about everything that I have suffered in my life; it all makes sense when I view it from this perspective. Everything was strategically planned to keep me distracted so that I would never recognize who I am in Christ and the purpose that I am to fulfill. I believe that most people who have been consistently attacked in life more than likely have a huge God-purpose and just haven't yet figured out how to "Fight for Their Purpose."

Jesus told a parable of a sower who sowed good seed in four different kinds of soils. I'm only going to focus on one kind of soil to make a point; you can read about the rest in your personal study time. The seed is the Word of God, as well as the prophetic promise, and Jesus is the One who sows the Truth into our hearts. The enemy comes along to plants weeds (worries, doubts, and distractions) to keep us from producing fruit and growing spiritually into all that Jesus planted in us.

Mark 4:18-19 tells the story: "The seed that fell among the

thorns represents others who hear God's word, but all too quickly the message is crowded out by the worries of this life, the lure of wealth, and the desire for other things, so no fruit is produced."

The spiritual cycle should be that the Word of God is sown or birthed in us and grows and matures in us to the point that we can plant it in the hearts of others. But the enemy clouds our minds and lives with worries and stress (which are fear based) to abort the fruitfulness of God in us. He knows that if we can ever get free enough, fruitful enough, and full of God's love, then signs and wonders will begin to follow us and we will pray for the sick and they will recover (Mark 16:18)!

It is important not to allow the cares of this world to choke out God's plan. Anxiety and worry drain us if we focus on them. Then we are weakened in our relationship with God.

Have you ever had a crazy situation occur right when you're getting closer to God or just when you step out in faith? It's not a coincidence, so keep focused, don't be distracted, and run to finish your race. Don't look to the left or right—keep your gaze on Jesus. Cross the threshold of destiny and do not get hindered by any attacks at the doorway. Move into your Promised Land!

I would like to use this illustration to explain how the enemy's distractions are sent to delay our destinies. You are sitting at the King's table because He said that He will spread a table for you in the presence of your enemies (Psalm 23:5). You are in fellowship with Jesus, the Bridegroom King Lover, enjoying His blessings, presence, love, and all of who He is, and your enemy is watching from the sidelines and recognizes that favor on your life. He will attack through anyone, anything, and any situation to try and get your mind off the King. He will tempt, jump, shout, and do anything to cause you to look away. The more you pour out your time, adoration, attention, and affection on Jesus, the more powerful you become against the enemy. You begin to look like Jesus. You are transformed by fellowshipping with Jesus, from Glory to Glory.

If you can keep your eyes and heart focused on the Lord, no matter what is happening around you, then distractions literally won't be able to distract you. It's like that saying, "If you don't mind, it don't matter." Realize that the moment a negative thought doesn't bother you anymore, that is the very moment the enemy has lost his attack power. In the next chapter, I will teach how to effectively fight the enemy, because you can't afford to allow distractions to get you spiritually clouded and off focus. You have a destiny to fulfill!

LIMITING GOD

Hebrews 3:12-14 warns, "Be careful then, dear brothers and sisters. Make sure that your own hearts are not evil and unbelieving, turning you away from the living God. You must warn each other every day, while it is still 'today,' so that none of you will be deceived by sin and hardened against God. For if we are faithful to the end, trusting God just as firmly as when we first believed, we will share in all that belongs to Christ."

Another huge roadblock that delays our life journeys is limiting God through unbelief and not trusting Him. We rob ourselves of the full blessings and promises of God when we limit Him. Without faith, it's impossible to please God (Hebrews 11:6). Anything that is not of faith is classified as sin (see Romans 14:23). The following are examples of arrested spiritual progress due to limiting God. Psalm 78:39-41 (KJV) explains, "Yea, they turned back and tempted God, and limited the Holy One of Israel." Mark 6:5 says, "And because of their unbelief, he couldn't do any miracles among them except to place his hands on a few sick people and heal them."

Do you limit God in your life? Is there anything you find yourself believing that is just not possible for you to accomplish? You can actually limit how much you allow God to use you because of your lack of faith. I don't know about you, but I don't want to settle for less than God's best. I certainly don't want to delay and limit God's intended plan for my life. So, don't put boundaries on your life's purpose! Don't assume that God can only do "so much" through you. Instead, have "crazy faith" to believe that God's possibilities for you are limitless!

> Numbers 23:19—"God is not a man, so he does not lie. He is not human, so he does not change his mind. Has he ever spoken and failed to act? Has he ever promised and not carried it through?"

> Isaiah 55:11—"It is the same with my word. I send it out, and it always produces fruit. It will accomplish all I want it to, and it will prosper everywhere I send it."

> Isaiah 40:8—"The grass withers and the flowers fade, but the word of our God stands forever."

If you are finding it really hard to trust God and believe the things that His Word says about you, then pray this prayer, just as a man prayed regarding the healing and deliverance of his son: "I believe Lord, but help my unbelief." If you are struggling, maybe because your journey of arriving to the prophetic promises of God has been very prolonged, then you may consider fasting and prayer. In the following Scripture, Jesus tells the disciples that this kind of "unbelief" can only come out through prayer and fasting. It is worth doing whatever it takes to get rid of doubt and unbelief, in order to take the limits off of what God wants to do in your life. As you see in this story, Jesus was willing to heal the boy; the disciples weren't able to because of their unbelief. Not because the demon was so powerful or the situation was so bad, but because their faith was shaken by what they were witnessing. They didn't have enough faith to carry out the will and desires of God. It is time to break any agreements with doubt and unbelief in Jesus' name.

"Then one of the crowd answered and said, 'Teacher, I brought You my son, who has a mute spirit. And wherever it seizes him, it throws him down; he foams at the mouth, gnashes his teeth, and becomes rigid. So I spoke to Your disciples, that they should cast it out, but they could not.' "He answered him and said, **'O faithless generation, how long shall I be with you? How long shall I bear with you? Bring him to Me.'** Then they brought him to Him. And when he saw Him, immediately the spirit convulsed him, and he fell on the ground and wallowed, foaming at the mouth.

"So He asked his father, 'How long has this been happening to him?' "And he said, 'From childhood. And often he has thrown him both into the fire and into the water to destroy him. But if You can do anything, have compassion on us and help us.'

"Jesus said to him, **'If you can believe, all things *are* possible to him who believes.'** "Immediately the father of the child cried out and said with tears, **'Lord, I believe; help my unbelief!'**

"When Jesus saw that the people came running together, He rebuked the unclean spirit, saying to it, 'Deaf and dumb spirit, I command you, come out of him and enter him no more!' Then *the spirit* cried out, convulsed him greatly, and came out of him. And he became as one dead, so that many said, 'He is dead.' But Jesus took him by the hand and lifted him up, and he arose.

"And when He had come into the house, His disciples asked Him privately, 'Why could we not cast it out?' So He said to them, 'This kind can come out by nothing but prayer and fasting.'" (Mark 9:17-29, NKJV, emphasis added)

WHAT YOU THINK AND SAY CAN CAUSE DELAY!

Stinking thinking is lethal! Thoughts and feelings turn into words and words become reality. If you constantly think counter-productive thoughts, then those thoughts will turn into counter-productive words and actions. If you believe the lie that you will never be everything that the Word says you are, then you are responsible for delaying God's Word from manifesting.

On a daily basis, the enemy personally attacks us by throwing negative thoughts at our minds; if we are not careful, these thoughts turn into negative feelings about ourselves. Lies, as we've talked about previously, are one of the enemy's main tactics against us. Just because a lie enters your thoughts, it doesn't mean it's your true feelings. Don't take ownership over the lies that the enemy throws. Don't allow shame to creep in just because bad thoughts or visuals come into your mind. Rebuke them in Jesus' name. The moment you start speaking and believing the lies of the enemy, you empower them to exist because of the authority, faith, and power you've just yielded and given up. Proverbs 18:21 admonishes, "The tongue can bring death or life; those who love to talk will reap the consequences."

The enemy knows that whatever we speak, we create. So, if you are constantly down on yourself and allowing negative thoughts to cycle through your mind, there's no way you can fulfill the plan God has for you. The enemy's goal is to get you to think negatively about yourself and to get you to confess negative things about yourself. Proverbs 23:7 says, "...For as he thinks in his heart, so is he" (AMP). Don't allow bad thoughts to hang out in your head.

Jesus overcame these things for us. After prayer and fasting in the wilderness for 40 days, the enemy tempted Him three times and threw twisted lies and visuals at Jesus. The third time, it says in Matthew 4:8, "Next the devil took him to the peak of a very high mountain and showed him all the kingdoms of the world and their glory. 'I will give it all to you,' he said, 'if you will kneel down and worship me.'"

So, Jesus was hearing the attacks of the enemy and He was also seeing the visuals of what the enemy was throwing at Him, yet Jesus defeated the enemy with the Word of God all three times. I share this story with you because sometimes thoughts or pictures may enter your head that the enemy throws at you like darts. But it is your shield of faith (Ephesians 6:10-18) that stops all of the darts of the enemy. It was what you really believe deep down inside that will determine what you allow to remain in your head, then spoken out of your mouth.

Keep applying truth and use your shield of faith to stop those lies from being planted and becoming part of you. If you are someone who has the supernatural gift of discernment and you pick up on things happening with people or in environments, these truths will be very helpful. Don't believe everything that gets thrown at your mind is yours. Don't feel shame about thoughts and visuals that aren't yours. Your own words could be hindering you. You speak what you believe, and your words set a course for you.

Proverbs 18:7 is a warning: "The mouths of fools are their ruin; they trap themselves with their lips." Recognize when negative thoughts come into your mind and change them! Ask God to help you think positive thoughts and speak positive things about yourself and your future. Positive affirmations and declarations are highly beneficial in retraining your thoughts and words. (Please refer back to Chapter 2.1 Self-Work.) If you don't have something nice to say about yourself, then don't say it.

SELF-WORK

After reading this chapter, does anything come to mind that could be delaying God's plan for your life?

_____
_____
_____
_____
_____
_____

What do you need to specifically work on to make sure that God's timing occurs as He desires in your life?

_____
_____
_____
_____
_____
_____

Again, what lies are you believing about yourself, your purpose, or God?

_____
_____
_____
_____
_____
_____

What areas do you struggle with lack of trust, unbelief, and doubt?

_____
_____
_____
_____
_____
_____

What unhealthy statements do you need to stop speaking?

_____
_____
_____
_____
_____
_____

2.8 THE FIGHT_

> "We use God's mighty weapons, not worldly weapons, to knock down the strongholds of human reasoning and to destroy false arguments. We destroy every proud obstacle that keeps people from knowing God. We capture their rebellious thoughts and teach them to obey Christ. And after you have become fully obedient, we will punish everyone who remains disobedient." (2 Corinthians 10:4-6)

Whether you know it or not, there is a spiritual war going on. The Bible says that this battle is not ours, it's the Lord's (2 Chronicles 20:15). God does not want us ignorant concerning the devices of the enemy (2 Corinthians 2:11). The enemy knows that God is absolutely in love with us because we are His children. He knows that God's will and power works through us, so Satan tries to ultimately kill, steal, and destroy our lives to prevent the will of God from coming to pass through us. We must be equipped and become aware of how to fight the good fight of faith and how to stand against the wiles of the enemy. This is critical in your ability to overcome every obstacle on your way to becoming what God created you to be.

Ephesians 6:10-17 admonishes us, "A final word: Be strong in the Lord and in his mighty power. Put on all of God's armor so that you will be able to stand firm against all strategies of the devil. For we are not fighting against flesh-and-blood enemies, but against evil rulers and authorities of the unseen world, against mighty powers in this dark world, and against evil spirits in the heavenly places. Therefore, put on every piece of God's armor so you will be able to resist the enemy in the time of evil. Then after the battle you will still be standing firm. Stand your ground, putting on the belt of truth and the body armor of God's righteousness. For shoes, put on the peace that comes from the Good News so that you will be fully prepared. In addition to all of these, hold up the shield of faith to stop the fiery arrows of the devil. Put on salvation as your helmet, and take the sword of the Spirit, which is the word of God."

If you attempt to find natural answers and methods to your spiritual problems, you will just end up frustrated. We just read in Ephesians 6:10-17 that our battle weapon, our sword, is the Word of God. Our defense when under attack is our shield of faith (what we really believe). When faith and the Word of God are used together along with the rest of the protective armor, we have a sure victory! Jesus has already won the fight. He died on the cross, was buried, and rose from the dead with ALL power in His hands. He shamed the enemy openly in His victory over him on the cross (Colossians 2:15). Now we are seated in Christ and have been given His authority in combat. The problem is that most of the time, we are clueless to how much authority we have and how to use the spiritual weapons we've already been given.

THE ENEMY'S BATTLE PLANS

The primary example of how to fight spiritual battles is seen in how Jesus dealt with the attacks of the enemy. He was not obsessively focused on the enemy, but as I mentioned before, the reason the enemy attacks us is not about us. He wants to prevent God's Kingdom from coming and God's will from being done. This was the reason for Satan's three specific attacks against Jesus right before He stepped out into full-time ministry to do the will of God and reveal the power of the Kingdom.

Matthew 4:1-11 says:

> "Then Jesus was led by the Spirit into the wilderness to be tempted there by the devil. For forty days and forty nights he fasted and became very hungry. During that time the devil came and said to him, 'If you are the Son of God, tell these stones to become loaves of bread.' But Jesus told him, No! The Scriptures say 'People do not live by bread alone, but by every word that comes from the mouth of God.' Then the devil took him to the holy city, Jerusalem, to the highest point of the Temple, and said, 'If you are the Son of God, jump off! For the Scriptures say, He will order his angels to protect you. And they will hold you up with their hands so you won't even hurt your foot on a stone.' Jesus responded, 'The Scriptures also say, You must not test the Lord your God.' Next the devil took him to the peak of a very high mountain and showed him all the kingdoms of the world and their glory. 'I will give it all to you,' he said, 'if you will kneel down and worship me.' 'Get out of here, Satan,' Jesus told him. 'For the Scriptures say, You must worship the Lord your God and serve only him.' Then the devil went away, and angels came and took care of Jesus."

The enemy came to attack Jesus at a very strategic time. He had just been baptized, audibly confirmed by God to be His Son, and the Holy Spirit had descended on Him. Not only did He know His life-purpose, but everyone that witnessed His baptism knew it. He then went into the wilderness to fast and pray before launching the full-time ministry for which He was brought to earth. Jesus knew God's voice over His life and the enemy was challenging what God said. The enemy came to Him with a vicious spiritual attack trying to cut Him off from fulfilling God's will on the earth. The enemy tried to use any human weakness he thought would give him leverage against Jesus. Satan, the ruler of this world (John 14:30), attacked Jesus with all of the same tricks he still uses today: the lust of the flesh, the lust of the eyes, and the pride of life.

First John 2:16 talks about these three tricks: "For the world offers only a craving for physical pleasure [turn these stones into bread], a craving for everything we see [all the kingdoms of the world], and pride in our achievements and possessions [if you are the Son of God, jump]. These are not from the Father, but are from this world" (bracketed words added).

Jesus had His full spiritual armor on and He was ready. He was wearing the helmet of salvation: He knew He belonged to God and no words of the enemy would twist His mindset. As He wore the breastplate of righteousness, He knew He was in right-standing with God and His heart was guarded. The belt of truth secured Him so He wouldn't fall for the lies of the enemy. His feet were ready to spread the Gospel through His ministry. His shield of faith blocked all the fiery darts of the enemy. Jesus fought with the sword of the Spirit, by quoting the Word of God.

THE DANGER OF BEING EMPTY

Jesus was prepared for the attacks that came. His continual defeat of the enemy empowers us to do the same. Often people get lazy in their approach to God, until something bad or challenging happens. There are some people who constantly deal with the same issues and the same demons over and over. The Lord forgives them, delivers them, and heals them, making them clean. However, because they are not filled with God's Word and the Holy Spirit, the enemy returns to tempt them with all the same junk. If they are not living yielded to the Lord, then they will more than likely act on the temptations presenting themselves and open the door to the enemy again. Being tempted is not a sin; even Jesus was tempted. However, the actions we take after the temptation determine if it leads to the act of sin.

Matthew 12:43-45 reveals, "When an evil spirit leaves a person, it goes into the desert, seeking rest but finding none. Then it says, 'I will return to the person I came from.' So it returns and finds its former home empty, swept, and in order. Then the spirit finds seven other spirits more evil than itself, and they all enter the person and live there. And so that person is worse off than before. That will be the experience of this evil generation."

Has God ever delivered you out of a crazy situation and you went right back to it, resulting in things being worse than they were the first time? Here's why: it's not enough to just get free, because we have to stay free! When you experience a victory over the struggles, it's imperative that you fill the newly clean and free places with God's Word and ask for the filling of the Holy Spirit. Daily seek Jesus for love encounters. It is such an adventurous joy to have encounters with Jesus. Focus on Him and deny all temptations and distractions that would try to steal your freedom.

Feed your spirit on a daily basis. Read the Bible, pray, praise and worship God. Dance, sing, create, write... Be intentional about encountering Jesus. Always be thankful and keep your mind stayed on Him. Galatians 6:8 warns, "Those who live only to satisfy their own sinful nature will harvest decay and death from that sinful nature. But those who live to please the Spirit will harvest everlasting life from the Spirit."

When you live a life surrendered to God, acknowledging Him in all that you do and walking in His ways, you will be less likely to fall into temptation. When you keep yourself spiritually full, you won't fall for the same old tricks of the enemy as easily. Not only this, but you will have more self-control when it comes to the flesh.

Galatians 5:16-17 teaches, "So I say, let the Holy Spirit guide your lives. Then you won't be doing what your sinful nature craves. The sinful nature wants to do evil, which is just the opposite of what the Spirit wants. And the Spirit gives us desires that are the opposite of what the sinful nature desires. These two forces are constantly fighting each other, so you are not free to carry out your good intentions."

WHY IS THE SWORD SO EFFECTIVE IN BATTLE?

- Hebrews 4:12 explains, "For the word of God is alive and powerful. It is sharper than the sharpest two-edged sword, cutting between soul and spirit, between joint and marrow. It exposes our innermost thoughts and desires."
- John 6:63 adds, "The Spirit alone gives eternal life. Human effort accomplishes nothing. And the very words I have spoken to you are spirit and life."
- Isaiah 55:11 emphasizes these things about the Word: "It is the same with my word. I send it out, and it always produces fruit. It will accomplish all I want it to, and it will prosper everywhere I send it."
- John 1:1-2 tells us, "In the beginning the Word already existed. The Word was with God, and the Word was God. He existed in the beginning with God."
- Matthew 24:35 makes the solid declaration, "Heaven and earth will disappear, but my words will never disappear."
- Finally, Numbers 23:19 assures us that, "God is not a man, so he does not lie. He is not human, so he does not change his mind. Has he ever spoken and failed to

act? Has he ever promised and not carried it through?"

THE WEAPONS OF PRAISE AND WORSHIP

The enemy hates praise and worship to God, because it's what that he wanted for himself. There is breakthrough power in our praise and worship. There may be a time when you have spoken God's Word to your situation, have prayed, and still have not received a breakthrough. Try praising and worshiping God with everything you've got! No matter what the circumstances appear to be, no matter how bad the attack, just take your eyes off of the issue and put your eyes, heart, and mind on God through praise and worship. Do it daily; put your favorite praise and worship songs on and spend time in His presence. It doesn't matter where you are. You could be at home, the car, or the bathroom stall at work. Sometimes you just have to break away and praise God to win the battle.

The Bible says God inhabits the praises of His people (Psalm 22:3). Since He lives in your praise, whenever you need God's supernatural presence to help you, just praise Him. Where the Spirit of the Lord is, there is freedom (2 Corinthians 3:17). There is freedom from temptation, sickness, and struggle in your praise and worship, because God dwells there. Praising God and worshiping Him are some of the last things your flesh wants to do when you are stressed, angry, or depressed. You must find a way to press into His glorious presence, for there you will find everything that you need.

WHAT THE BIBLE SAYS ABOUT THE WEAPON OF PRAYER

- Mark 11:24-25—"I tell you, you can pray for anything, and if you believe that you've received it, it will be yours. But when you are praying, first forgive anyone

you are holding a grudge against, so that your Father in heaven will forgive your sins, too."
- Philippians 4:6—"Don't worry about anything; instead, pray about everything. Tell God what you need, and thank him for all he has done."
- James 5:13-14—"Are any of you suffering hardships? You should pray. Are any of you happy? You should sing praises. Are any of you sick? You should call for the elders of the church to come and pray over you, anointing you with oil in the name of the Lord."
- Matthew 26:41—"Keep watch and pray, so that you will not give in to temptation. For the spirit is willing, but the body is weak!"
- Matthew 7:7—"Keep on asking, and you will receive what you ask for. Keep on seeking, and you will find. Keep on knocking, and the door will be opened to you."
- James 5:16—"Confess your sins to each other and pray for each other so that you may be healed. The earnest prayer of a righteous person has great power and produces wonderful results."
- Jude 1:20—"But you, dear friends, must build each other up in your most holy faith, pray in the power of the Holy Spirit..."
- Romans 8:26-27—"And the Holy Spirit helps us in our weakness. For example, we don't know what God wants us to pray for. But the Holy Spirit prays for us with groanings that cannot be expressed in words. And the Father who knows all hearts knows what the Spirit is saying, for the Spirit pleads for us believers in harmony with God's own will."

WARRING FROM THE PLACE OF INTIMACY WITH JESUS

Song of Solomon (Song of Songs) is one of my favorite books of the Bible. The Passion Translation transformed my life into deeper revelation of love between Jesus and the Bride. I encourage you to read this book. One of the beautiful revelations found within is the concept of warfare from the place of intimacy with Jesus, seated with Him in heavenly realms, as Ephesians 2:6 also mentions. Sometimes we can feel so overwhelmed by the attacks of the enemy, and the strategy of the Lord is to ascend with Him and just be loved by Him. Everything else seems to dissipate when you are in a love encounter with Jesus. Nothing else matters.

> "Every part of you is so beautiful, my darling. Perfect is your beauty, without flaw within. Now you are ready, my bride, to come with me as we climb the highest peaks together. Come with me through the archway of trust. We will look down from the crest of the glistening mounts and from the summit of our sublime sanctuary. **Together we will wage war** in the lion's den and the leopard's lair as they watch nightly for their prey. For you reach into my heart. With one flash of your eyes I am undone by your love, my beloved, my equal, my bride. You leave me breathless—I am overcome by merely a glance from your worshiping eyes, for you have stolen my heart. I am held hostage by your love and by the graces of righteousness shining upon you. How satisfying to me, my equal, my bride. Your love is my finest wine—intoxicating and thrilling. And your sweet, perfumed praises—so exotic, so pleasing." (Song of Songs 4:7-10 TPT)

I love how Jesus leads the Bride through an archway of trust in a high place, where together they wage war. She is not warring alone, but with Him, fully trusting Him. Reading on, the Bridegroom King Lover's style of warfare is lavishing His love upon the Bride. I'm sure the Bride is not consumed by the war when hearing His love-drenched words of affection toward her. Let the reality of this revelation be yours, the place that you now view fighting the enemy from. Lean into encounters with Jesus and ask Him to speak to you. Everything is put into the right perspective from here. Ask Him to reveal Himself to you and give you the grace to ascend with Him above all of the attacks and warfare of the enemy. Ask Him to help you to fully trust Him through it all.

Using these tools will help you through every fight. Follow the example of Jesus: operate in God's love, understand your spiritual armor and authority, and use the Word of God as your sword. Stay full of God's Word and be filled with His Spirit. Praise and worship God daily. Continually be in prayer, speaking to God and keeping your ears open to hear from Him. Pursue intimate encounters with Jesus. Feed your spiritual side and not your flesh!

SELF-WORK

In what areas of your life do you feel that you are fighting right now?

_____

Are there any specific struggles or attacks that are recurring in your life? Ask Jesus why.

_____
_____
_____
_____
_____

Which tools or weapons do you need to use more when fighting?

_____
_____
_____
_____
_____

What's your game plan for being more effective in battle?

_____
_____
_____
_____
_____

2.9 THE PREP TIME_

"But he knows where I am going. And when he tests me, I will come out as pure as gold." (Job 23:10)

The preparation process leading up to living out your full God-potential is extremely important. Your prep time is the foundation for your success. This is a beautiful time to allow the Lord to examine your heart and to give you practical and spiritual lessons that bring maturity. Be humble and teachable. There are several examples in the Word of people who went through this process: David, Esther, Moses, Joseph, Paul, and Jesus Himself, who had thirty years of preparation before stepping into three years of full-time ministry.

I was about 16 when God first revealed to me that I had a calling on my life. I remember wanting to instantly travel the world and do everything that God showed me I would do. I felt like I was ready, so why couldn't I just jump into full-time ministry and accomplish it all right away? I was on fire with passion and zeal to do whatever God wanted me to do. Now when I look back, there's no way that I could have done it all then; I was clueless and didn't realize it. The prep time is 100% necessary. I had the passion, but I did not have the healing, character, or the wisdom yet. Matthew 25:4 tells us that the wise are prepared. Now this doesn't mean that you can't immediately be used in ministry by God right after salvation. You can absolutely share your faith, evangelize, and see the healing miracles, signs, and wonders of the Kingdom from day one. Preparation and humility to learn and grow is vital to bearing fruit that remains.

God's preparation is a pruning, refining, renewing, and learning process; it is a time of character development and of gaining maturity. In fact, I believe that we will be students forever, continually learning and growing in every season.

Philippians 4:6 (NKJV) directs us to "Be anxious for nothing, but in everything by prayer and supplication, with thanksgiving, let your requests be made known to God." You must be patient during your prep time and realize that patience is a virtue and part of the fruit of the Spirit. In God's perfect timing, He will bring the big opportunities that will launch you to His ultimate destination for you. You do not want to try and get ahead of God to make things happen on your own. The last thing you want to do is make decisions based on the fleshly ideas of your own understanding or emotions. That never leads anywhere good. I heard someone once say that whatever you establish in the flesh will have to be maintained in the flesh. That would be absent of God's power, wisdom, direction, protection, and supernatural grace. In order for God to get the most impact out of your life, for you to reach the pinnacle of your life's success in Him, you must choose to allow your life to be led by God (Spirit-led).

TAKING ADVANTAGE OF TIME

The sound advice found in 2 Timothy 2:15 says, "Work hard so you can present yourself to God and receive his approval. Be a good worker, one who does not need to be ashamed and who correctly explains the word of truth." Don't just wait around for opportunities to come your way. Research and study everything you can in order to gain expertise in the area of your purpose. Study your life purpose as if you were in college for it, if you are not already pursuing education in that area, which is wise. Look for ways to volunteer or work in the field of your life purpose. Surround yourself with people who can mentor you, because they are already doing what you are aspiring to do. However, be careful not to go after friendships and relationships with false motives of personal gain. Allow God to show you the people He wants you aligned with. Take the prep time seriously!

Habakkuk 2:2 (NKJV) says, "Then the Lord answered me and said: 'Write the vision and make it plain on tablets, That he may run who reads it.'" Write out the dream God has given you. Keep it in front of you at home, school, and on your job; take little reminders with you of the vision God has for you. This is a special time of seeking the Lord for prophetic glimpses of His plan so that when the time is right, you have clarity from heaven on the steps that you are to take. Ask God for wisdom, knowledge, understanding, and sensitivity to revelation from Holy Spirit. Keep yourself passionate about where you are going in Him. Pray and create an action plan with the Lord, including goals to work toward. Of course, the plan is always subject to change at any moment by the Lord, but you should always be moving toward something. Create an inspiring environment around yourself and seek out resources that will help you achieve the vision.

I've personally seen people who appear to have no initiative in the very area that they say that God has called them to work in. It can't be assumed that ministry opportunities will come easily, like "a pie in the sky." I can't speak for any other field, but in ministry, it's the one who is consistently volunteering, faithfully serving, and humbly involved with a great positive attitude, that usually is placed into a ministry position. It is not the person just waiting around for a ministry to be handed to them. I can't even count the times that people have said, "I want to get involved and do ministry," yet they refuse to be a greeter or do something as simple as pull up weeds when needed, and taking out the trash is below them. They want to get into the pulpit to preach and don't realize that it's only five to ten percent of the pastor's job! Most of the work is behind the scenes and not everyone wants to do the behind- the-scenes work that it takes to be used up front by God. Many are called, but few are chosen (Matthew 22:14).

THE CONDITION OF YOUR HEART DURING PREPARATION

"But the Lord said to Samuel, 'Don't judge by his appearance or height, for I have rejected him. The Lord doesn't see things the way you see them. People judge by outward appearance, but the Lord looks at the heart.'" (1 Samuel 16:7)

Do not be discouraged when others receive the things that you want and desire. Don't look at the outward appearance judging what you think they deserve or don't deserve. The Lord looks at the heart. Here are a few questions for you that may or may not relate...

- Have you been complaining, negative, frustrated, prideful or jealous?
- Have you procrastinated and ignored obeying the voice of God in certain areas?
- Have you consciously continued engaging in sin that the Lord has personally asked you to step away from?
- Do you have a long list of people that you refuse to forgive?
- Do you find yourself being very critical of others and continually have an opinion about them?

Sometimes, we can easily fall for the temptation of thinking these things are acceptable, not realizing that they are heart flaws that will prevent success. There is grace, healing, and freedom through Christ as you have read in previous chapters. So, don't let shame or condemnation creep in right now. But turn your heart toward the Lord and repent for anything that you feel like has kept you out of God's timing and next steps for your life.

Moving forward, when someone else gets the promotion or position that you've been dreaming about, don't talk negatively about the leadership or management because they didn't pick you. Sincerely celebrate with that person and stay positive. When others get opportunities or things that you have been desperately believing God for, praise the Lord in faith, knowing that the same God who did it for them can do it for you. Shift your perspective to the GOODNESS OF GOD. You have to believe that He is good to you and has a beautiful plan for your life. Promotion doesn't come from leadership or people; promotion comes from God!

Psalm 75:6-7 (AMP) explains, "For not from the east nor from the west nor from the south come promotion and lifting up. But God is the Judge! He puts down one and lifts up another."

In other words, don't blame the pastor, your boss, or the investor if you don't get chosen. Continue being faithful in your preparation process and God will exalt you in due time. You absolutely don't want to be given an opportunity that you don't have the skill or character to handle. It would be horrible to be given the opportunity that you have been striving for, only to lose it due to being unable to handle the stress that comes with the opportunity... or not having the strength to turn away from temptations and attacks that surround the position... or maybe not having your priorities in order and somehow losing your grip on the things that matter most to you in life... or even losing your passion and pursuit of God once you got what you wanted. These are examples of pitfalls people face when they are not prepared enough, mature enough, or prayed up enough to handle new success. Many rise in fame, but fall even faster than they rose. You want to be able to maintain and mature in what God gives you.

Matthew 6:33 (NKJV) advises, "But seek first the kingdom of God and His righteousness, and all these things shall be added to you." Keep your heart and mind focused on living from the Kingdom reality and on living in the righteousness (purity) of Christ. When our heart is to advance the Kingdom and remain pure through Jesus, everything we need in life will be given to us. Keep your heart pure before Him; don't allow anything to get you off track or distract you during the season of preparation. This is the time that you are "in school," learning important lessons for the rest of your life. Take every chance you get to have "God-learning" moments. When you know that you have been doing as much as you can on your part while walking in obedience, just be still in the presence of the Lord and wait patiently for Him to act (Psalm 37:7).

PREPARATION WISDOM

One of the things you should continually pray for is wisdom. "If you need wisdom, ask our generous God, and He will give it to you. He will not rebuke you for asking" (James 1:5). Wisdom is God's "know-how." His wisdom will reveal which decision to make and what steps to take. This is part of being led by God, as I mentioned earlier. When you don't know what to do as you prepare to be all God created you to be, ask for wisdom. We should all aspire to be people of wisdom.

Lessons from the Wise:

- Proverbs 12:23—Wise people don't make a show of their knowledge.
- Proverbs 14:16—Wise people are cautious and avoid danger.
- Proverbs 21:22—Wise people conquer the strong man and level his defenses.

- Proverbs 9:8—Wise people receive correction.
- Proverbs 10:8—Wise people are glad to be instructed.
- Proverbs 15:7—Wise people give good advice.
- Proverbs 12:15—Wise people take advice from others.
- Proverbs 16:21—Wise people are known for their understanding.
- Proverbs 29:11—Wise people quietly hold back their anger.
- Proverbs 24:5—Wise people are mightier than the strong, and those with knowledge grow stronger and stronger.

TRUST GOD AND DELIGHT IN HIM

Finally, trust God on this journey. He is the one who created you and He wants you to succeed even more than you do. This is His plan and it happens in His timing. Trust Him. Stay sensitive to His voice leading you. Remain humble with a good attitude and ask for help when you need it. Know and believe that God will lead you through this time of preparation and bring you to the exact place that you are supposed to be, if you let Him. Philippians 1:6 encourages, "And I am certain that God, who began the good work within you, will continue his work until it is finally finished on the day when Christ Jesus returns."

SELF-WORK

Write out the vision or God-goal that you have in your heart.

_____
_____
_____
_____
_____
_____

How are you going to keep this in front of you?

_____
_____
_____
_____
_____
_____

What specific things do you need to educate yourself?

_____
_____
_____
_____
_____
_____

Is there anything in your heart that needs adjusted during your prep time?

_____
_____
_____
_____
_____
_____

2.10 THE ALIGNMENT_

"To the fatherless he is a father. To the widow he is a champion friend. To the lonely he makes them part of a family. To the prisoners he leads into prosperity until they sing for joy. This is our Holy God in his Holy Place! But for the rebels there is heartache and despair." (Psalm 68:5-6 TPT)

We were created for family with Father God, Jesus, Holy Spirit, and fellow believers. The truth is that the body of Christ is structured in a way that we need each other. There is great joy and adventure in being together. Why is it that the "more spiritual" people get, the more they think they don't need anyone's help? Or that they know it all and have nothing to learn from others? You will need to be aligned with people that can help you find and fulfill God's plan. Once you are in God's plan, you need others to be a blessing in your personal life to keep you growing, humble, and healthy.

So many times, in the Word, we see God's people led and mentored by others in their walk with God. Form godly relationships with others and find someone who you can be 100% real with, who can pray for you, and who can give you biblical advice. Accountability is healthy and productive. Sometimes we think more highly of ourselves than we ought to and we need someone to help us find humility. An outsider's view into your life will help you and sharpen you in more ways than you know. Apart from God and His family, there is loneliness, heartache, and despair. It is not Father God's plan for you to be lonely.

Jesus aligned Himself with a team of twelve disciples to help Him accomplish the will of God; He is our Example. The Bible says that a servant is no greater than his master (John 13:16). If Jesus got help and strategically formed a group of people around Him, then we should, too. I'm not saying that you have to go and find 12 disciples, but I am just stressing the importance of community and building godly relationships. We can accomplish mighty exploits for the Lord with His aligned family, in the Body of Christ, moving in agreement by faith, as we co-labor with Jesus for His Glory.

CIRCLE OF INFLUENCE

Which way are you being swayed by the people around you? What is your circle of influence and who is a part of it? Do the people you're around encourage you to obey God or pull you away from Him? The way that you answer that question will be the deciding factor in keeping certain friends and relationships.

There will always be three types of people in your life: people that God uses, neutral people, and people that the enemy uses. Think about all of the relationships in your life right now. Who is good at encouraging you to fulfill your God-purpose? With whom do you interact that you know will hinder what God desires to accomplish in you? You can't afford to keep close friends or relationships that are damaging to your God-purpose. This can be a very hard reality, especially if you're realizing right now that you love the person or people who are toxic and not good for you. I am not saying that you shouldn't be going out into the world to win souls and make disciples. Of course, we should always be a light that reaches people in dark places. But what I am talking about is the people who are the closest to you, the people that you spend time with and interact with the most, the people who you have no walls with and communicate with daily.

"Yes Men" do not make the best inner circle friends. You don't want someone who will just always agree with you, but you do need someone with godly character who will always tell you the truth. You don't need the justifications on sin and fleshly desires to be validated by people who will agree that it's "okay" to continually make bad decisions. Hebrews 3:13 advises us to "Help each other. Speak day after day to each other while it is still today so your heart will not become hard by being fooled by sin."

CONNECTION WITH THE FAMILY OF GOD

> "Every believer was faithfully devoted to following the teachings of the apostles. Their hearts were mutually linked to one another, sharing communion and coming together regularly for prayer. A deep sense of holy awe swept over everyone, and the apostles performed many miraculous signs and wonders. All the believers were in fellowship as one body, and they shared with one another whatever they had." (Acts 2:42-44 TPT)

Since Christians are all part of the family of God and we need each other, it is important to be part of a church. The type of church doesn't really matter, as long as the complete Truth is being taught and you really feel like you're at home. Miracles happen when we are together. If you do not currently have a church home, find one. When you find that church, join a small group (discipleship) and get involved in the ministries of the church. As you do that, God will connect you with Christians that will help you along your life journey. We all need that support system, whether we know it or not.

Here is an important concept: you are just one connection away from breaking through into the next season of your life. Even if you are a mature believer who has attained great wealth and success in life, you need to be a part of the church family. I believe there are some levels of increase in the Spirit and in the natural that only happen when we serve and give to others. The leadership of Jesus was based on serving. Breakthrough happens when the Bride of Christ, the Family of God, is together in unity. Hebrews 10:25 admonishes, "Let us not stay away from church meetings. Some people are doing this all the time. Comfort each other as you see the day of His return coming near."

Sometimes when going through life's situations, we have a tendency as human beings to think we can handle our problems all by ourselves. But if you don't have to, why would you want to? There are people that have been through times exactly like what you are living through today and they are now victorious. Don't allow pride to settle in and separate you from those that God can use to make a major difference in your life.

Find someone that knows how to pray and give you godly advice based on Scriptural wisdom. James 5:16 advises, "Tell your sins to each other. And pray for each other so you may be healed. The prayer from the heart of a man right with God has much power."

If you are insecure and compare yourself to others, you will really have difficulty connecting with people who actually have the ability to help you. Seek to build relationships with people who are already doing what you desire to do. Celebrate their victories, ask for their advice, look at their lives, and ask them how they got where they are, but don't compare yourself to them. Second Corinthians 10:12 reveals the right mindset: "We do not compare ourselves with those who think they are good. They compare themselves with themselves. They decide what they think is good or bad and compare themselves with those ideas. They are foolish."

THE TRICK OF ISOLATION

"Divide and conquer" seems to be a recurring theme in the enemy's attack against Christians. Isolation is one of his strategies to weaken believers and position them to be more vulnerable. The ultimate goal of the enemy is to not only separate individuals from other believers, but then to separate them from God. I have fallen for this trick many times in my life. My hurts, traumas, and sins created the right atmosphere for the temptation to become isolated.

The thoughts that would come to me were, "No one understands what I'm going through; they are just going to judge or reject me. My problems are just too shameful to talk about." All of that negative self-talk and lying darts from the enemy would usually result in leaving the church or separating from believers. That is the worst thing to do when you need help! Before you know it, you're not connected to life-giving people or a life-giving church. It becomes easier to be tempted by the world and the enemy, to self-medicate your pain, and to put your trust in anything but God. Don't fall for this trick! Please don't make the mistake of thinking God is like the people who have mistreated you and run from Him. In John 15:5, Jesus said, "I am the Vine and you are the branches. Get your life from Me. Then I will live in you and you will give much fruit. You can do nothing without Me."

Have you ever noticed that the people who are very easily offended will find just one thing the pastor says during a sermon and then leave the church? Offense can be one of the first steps to isolation if you let it distract you from the big picture. If you are someone who gets offended easily and always gets your feelings hurt, you've got to get that under the blood of Jesus, because that merely creates division between you and the people who can help you most. Offense will rob you of family, success, and intimacy with God. If that is something that you have struggled with, take a moment to pray and surrender that to the Lord. Ask Him, "Jesus, do I struggle with being easily offended, do I agree with offense easily?" Then pray, "Father, I repent for offense, judgment, criticism, and false discernment. I renounce any lies that I have believed through offense. I choose to forgive anyone who has offended me in the past. What truth do You want to reveal to me, Lord?"

POURING INTO OTHERS

> "We have much to say about this topic although it is difficult to explain, because you have become too dull and sluggish to understand. For you should already be professors instructing others by now; but instead, you need to be taught from the beginning the basics of God's prophetic oracles! You're like children still needing milk and not yet ready to digest solid food. For every spiritual infant who lives on milk is not yet pierced by the revelation of righteousness. But solid food is for the mature, whose spiritual senses perceive *heavenly matters.* And they have been adequately trained by what they've experienced to emerge with understanding of the difference between what is truly excellent and what is evil and harmful." (Hebrews 5:11-14 TPT)

To bring balance to the other side of alignment, not only do we need others, but other people need us. We should all eventually grow to a place of maturity where we are pouring into and teaching others. This prevents us from getting "dull and sluggish." As we are praying into who God wants us to be aligned with, it is also a great idea to consider who you can pour into. The solid food of the "meat" and Word of God is digested by personal hunger, revelation, and understanding that comes from relationship with Jesus. The Lord does not want us to stay in a place of nursing infancy where we only receive "milk" through the revelation of others. Whatever we give away increases in the Kingdom of God. What we sow, we reap.

A great strategy is to give away what you personally need. If alignment with people who can mother and father you to the next level is what you need, then offer that to someone else and help them in the areas that you already have victory. Don't just sit around crying in self-pity, believing the lie that no one sees you or values you; give value to others. The reward of the smile on the face of Jesus for serving and loving His people is the most satisfying delight of the soul. Pray about ministries, organizations, agencies, and businesses that you could serve and learn from... or pour out and invest into. What you give away, and steward well, increases.

A favorite scripture to many is Nehemiah 8:10, "The joy of the Lord is your strength." This scripture, in context, is referring to believers "assembled with a unified purpose" (Nehemiah 8:1). They had just completed building the wall around Jerusalem. Gathered in agreement, they heard God's word then feasted & celebrated together. They were aligned for a God Purpose... Valuing God's Word because they heard it and understood it. So, there is joy and strength from the Lord in being aligned with believers for His Purpose.

PRAY FOR ALIGNMENT

Pray that God will put the right people into your life and that He will keep you sensitive to His connections with others, connections that may be vital to your personal process and success. Pray for spiritual family, business professionals, prayer warriors, mentors, and others who can help you to be brought into your life. You may have someone already in your life that God can use to bring fulfillment to His will for you. Pray that He would reveal people to you that will help you find your purpose. Pray for discernment and the ability to see the motives and hearts of those in your inner circle. Ask the Lord who you should be pouring into. Also, pray that God would remove anyone who would be unhealthy or used by the enemy to sabotage your progress. Trust God; He will do it!

SELF-WORK

Who do you know that could help you reach your God-goals?

_____
_____
_____
_____
_____

To whom could you go to for prayer and godly counsel?

_____
_____
_____
_____
_____

Who do you know that is already living out what you dream of doing? Ask the Lord how you can learn from their life, ministry, business, or organization.

_____
_____
_____
_____
_____
_____

2.11 THE DREAM_

Living the dream is all about pleasing the Lord with our surrendered life of intimacy with Him and obedience to His voice. Personally, my greatest reward is sensing the smile of Jesus, encountering Him, seeing His face. In the "dream" moments of my life, the greatest part to me is being with the Lord after accomplishing something for Him, when no one is looking, alone with Jesus. I have found that JESUS IS MY REWARD. Encountering Him brings me into holy experiences of ecstasy in His Glory. He satisfies my soul like nothing else in this world. Delighting and rejoicing in Him, with Him, makes my soul complete. Encountering Jesus should be our ultimate dream. We should place our treasures and investments into ways to encounter Him more.

As we lean into Jesus through prayer, worship, reading His Word, waiting on Him, listening, watching, abiding... He begins speaking prophetically to us about things to come. You will get visions, glimpses, instruction, direction, wisdom, and steps to take. There are dreams for your life within the heart of God to be revealed to you. Father God, Jesus, and Holy Spirit will empower you to live it out. Every day of our lives has been recorded in a heavenly book, His dreams, plans, and desires for us. Enjoy the following Scripture:

> "Lord, you know everything there is to know about me. You perceive every movement of my heart and soul, and you understand my every thought before it even enters my mind. You are so intimately aware of me, Lord. You read my heart like an open book and you know all the words I'm about to speak before I even start a sentence! You know every step I will take before my journey even begins. You've gone into my future to prepare the way, and in kindness you follow behind me to spare me from the harm of my past. With your hand of love upon my life, you impart a blessing to me. This is just too wonderful, deep, and incomprehensible! Your understanding of me brings me wonder and strength. Where could I go from your Spirit? Where could I run and hide from your face? If I go up to heaven, you're there! If I go down to the realm of the dead, you're there too! If I fly with wings into the shining dawn, you're there! If I fly into the radiant sunset, you're there waiting! Wherever I go, your hand will guide me; your strength will empower me. It's impossible to disappear from you or to ask the darkness to hide me, for your presence is everywhere, bringing light into my night. There is no such thing as darkness with you. The night, to you, is as bright as the day; there's no difference between the two. You formed my innermost being, shaping my delicate inside and my intricate outside, and wove them all together in my mother's womb. I thank you, God, for making me so mysteriously complex! Everything you do is marvelously breathtaking. It simply amazes me to think about it! How thoroughly you know me, Lord! You even formed every bone in my body when you created me in the secret place, carefully, skillfully shaping me from nothing to something. You saw who you created me to be before I became me! Before I'd ever seen the light of day, the number of days you planned for me were

already recorded in your book. Every single moment you are thinking of me! How precious and wonderful to consider that you cherish me constantly in your every thought! O God, your desires toward me are more than the grains of sand on every shore! When I awake each morning, you're still with me." (Psalm 139:1-18, TPT)

In my opinion, success is not measured by money, houses, cars, and plaques on the wall, but by how well we love Jesus. As we live in love with Him, we begin to look, sound, think, and speak more like Him. Our character is vital in living out our God-purpose.

When you arrive at a place in life that makes you feel like you are "living the dream," there are a few characteristics that you must have in order to succeed in maintaining that God-given success. Several people reach the height of their God-dreams, careers, ministries, and don't have the ability to stay there. They are like a shooting star that appears quickly and fades out just as fast as they appeared. You don't want to spend your life trying to find God's plan and fighting for your purpose, only to "blow it all" once you reach the place of fulfilling His will. A lifetime of preparation can possibly be lost in a moment of sin. Of course, God redeems, but why go through falling and the struggle of rebuilding? You can't stop working on yourself, nor can you quit seeing the need to mature and grow.

If you are accomplishing God's will to your fullest capacity, then you will be making a major dent in the kingdom of darkness. You have power and authority over the enemy, but that doesn't mean that Satan has stopped looking for opportunities to take you out. You don't want to step out of God's will at any time in life, but especially not when you are living the dream you've worked so hard to attain. Here is a principle to remember: great responsibility comes with living the dream. Consider the sobering words of Luke 12:48b: "When someone has been given much, much will be required in return; and when someone has been entrusted with much, even more will be required."

CHARACTER MUST HAVES

The following are character "must haves." These are the qualities needed to stay "in sync" with God and continue growing and expanding in His success.

1. INTEGRITY

Proverbs 10:9 says, "People with integrity walk safely, but those who follow crooked paths will slip and fall." Your honesty and godly character are essential components of the foundation that every area of work for the Lord is built upon. Whatever it is that you are to accomplish in life must be anchored in integrity if you desire to continually grow in success. The level of excellence seen in your everyday tasks should be honorable and pleasing to God. Luke 16:10 says, "If you are faithful in little things, you will be faithful in large ones. But if you are dishonest in little things, you won't be honest with greater responsibilities."

2. OBEDIENCE

The Bible says that obedience is better than sacrifice (1 Samuel 15:22). One of the ways Jesus said that He knows you love Him is if you do what He commands (John 14:15). Remain sensitive to the direction of God; always choose to obey Him quickly. No matter what pressure you may be under, obedience will keep you on the right path.

3. HUMILITY

Proverbs 16:18 warns, "Pride goes before destruction, and haughtiness before a fall." Never get caught up in the fame and glory of success and begin to think that it's all about you. Keep a humble nature. Don't let money change you. Do not let your power, influence with people, or titles and promotion change you... the list could go on and on. If you want to continue to live God's dream for your life, then humility is a must.

4. OFFENSE FREE

If you have unresolved issues with people, you must lay your gift down at the altar and be reconciled with them (Matthew 5:23-24). This means that God thinks that it is more important for you to be clear of drama, offenses, judgements, criticism, and unforgiveness with people, than it is for you to give your finances and your talents to Him. Forgiveness is extremely important! Don't let unforgiveness keep you from the blessings and favor of God on your endeavors. In fact, you must forgive if you want to be forgiven (Luke 6:37). Holding grudges equals carrying excess baggage and you need to be free when living the dream. The person who quickly forgives and lives unoffended guards their heart well. The enemy is very attracted to the sticky place of offense and unforgiveness. It can turn into bitterness, deep emotional pain, confusion, anger, feeling continually rejected, illness of the body and mind, etc. We've discussed this in previous chapters, but it is vital in living out our God-dreams.

5. PEACE

Philippians 4:7 encourages Christians to let the peace of God guard their hearts and minds. God's peace has the ability to protect your emotions and thoughts. Remaining in peace is one of the best things you can do for yourself. Don't allow life to get so busy that you are scattered, worn out, and making poor decisions. Peace is actually a tool that you can use as a deciding factor when faced with huge decisions. Colossians 3:15 says, "And let the peace that comes from Christ rule in your hearts. For as members of one body you are called to live in peace. And always be thankful." If you don't feel peace about doing something, don't do it. The peace of God will protect you and lead you.

6. FOCUS

Never move your focus away from Jesus. Peter found out the hard way, when he stepped out in faith to accomplish the miraculous. The moment he lost his focus on the Lord, he began to sink (Matthew 14:22-33). If you take your eyes off Jesus, you too will sink. He must always be the focus of your life's motives, passion, and purpose. Don't get to the point of thinking you can do it without Him. You can do nothing without Him. He is the vine and we are the branches. If we want to bear the most fruit and success possible, then we must stay connected to Him (John 15:1-17). Additionally, I would like to remind you of Matthew 6:33, which says, "Seek the Kingdom of God above all else, and live righteously, and he will give you everything you need." Seeking Jesus and His Kingdom requires intentional focus and pursuit.

7. BALANCE

Spending time with God, family, work, ministry, health, personal time... there are so many things to juggle! Keeping your priorities in order and balancing your life will eliminate a lot of chaos. Maintaining a detailed calendar can really help keep all of the compartments of your life in balance. When any of these areas of your life become neglected, problems are more than likely to arise. For example, don't make the mistake of putting work or ministry before your marriage. Come up with a game plan using a weekly schedule that ensures you are keeping balance in all the areas of your life. This is something that will always need attention because life is always changing. As seasons change, we have to be intentional about making room for the things that are important. Do not feel guilty for taking the time that you need to rest, exercise, or take care of your health. Burnout and stress have a way of affecting the body even when every other area of life seems to be going well. Balance is key.

8. PURITY

James 4:7 directs us, "Resist the Devil and he will flee from you." Temptations will come to distract you from your purpose. Remember, sin is never worth giving up everything for which you have worked. Your sins will find you out (Numbers 32:23); this means that everything that is secret will eventually be brought into the open, and everything that is concealed will be brought to light and known to all (Luke 8:17). If you have an area of weakness, you must be intentional about keeping yourself protected from it. Exposure is one of the greatest things you can do when you're being tempted; by this I mean that you should tell a spouse, friend, or mentor if you find yourself being tempted in a specific area. It is not a sin to be tempted; however, it is a sin to follow through and act on that temptation. Even Jesus was tempted, so don't conceal a temptation you're privately struggling with because of shame. Ask someone to pray with you about what is attempting to lure you; exposure will disarm the enemy and make you victorious.

9. BE A WORSHIPER

It's easy to forget to give God all of the glory. He deserves all the credit for every beautiful thing in our lives. It all comes from Him and, realistically, it all belongs to Him. We must be people who continuously deflect the praise and compliments of people toward the Lord. There will be seasons where you find it hard to spend time in praise and worship; those are the times we have to press in the most! God looks for those who will worship Him in spirit and in truth (John 4:23). We are created for relationship with Him and He is our greatest reward. Time in His presence is more valuable than anything else in our lives. If you haven't discovered this for yourself, then I hope that you become curious and very hungry to experience His presence. If you know the experience of encountering Him, then I pray that you never lose the desire to passionately pursue Him. That pursuit is truly our greatest life journey. We must worship Him in every season.

10. JOY AND CHILDLIKE FAITH

Childlike faith, awe, and wonder is a powerful strategy from heaven. This is the revelation that broke me through into seeing healing miracles in everyday life. As we believe God and dream big, we need to keep our hearts in the place of adventure and total dependence of Him. We can get so serious in life that we lose our ability to create with God. I heard someone once say that our load bearing capacity is directly related the amount of joy we have, because the joy of the Lord is our strength (Nehemiah 8:10). We must change our mindset from, "I know it all" to "Yay, God, teach me more!"

> "Learn this well: Unless you dramatically change your way of thinking and become teachable, and learn about heaven's kingdom realm with the wide-eyed wonder of a child, you will never be able to enter in. Whoever continually humbles himself to become like this gentle child is the greatest one in heaven's kingdom realm." (Matthew 18:3-4 TPT)

At the end of the day, it's all about bringing people to Jesus and God's will being done on earth as it is in heaven. It's not just about reaching your God-dream for yourself, it is also for every person who can find Him, through you living out that dream. Opposition will come and it won't always be easy. Don't allow the enemy to prevent you from God's plan. That is where and why the resistance comes: you have to fight for your purpose. You can't give up, because there are people that need to hear your story, people that you were designed to reach. You were born on your specific birthday to impact this generation and culture. There is so much more in you than you know. You were made for more!

In reading this book, I hope that you have become more aware of the potential, authority, power, gifts, and purpose within you. It has taken a large portion of my life to discover the simple truths within these pages; now you have it in the quick read of a book. With God, nothing is impossible for you! Look at my life and the things I've been through... if God can transform me and find value in me, then just imagine what He can do through you!

Philemon 1:6 (AMP) is my prayer for you: "[And I pray] that the participation in and sharing of your faith may produce and promote full recognition and appreciation and understanding and precise knowledge of every good [thing] that is ours in [our identification with] Christ Jesus [and unto His glory]."

SELF-WORK

If you were to pick one thing that could take you down, once you're living your God-dream, what would it be? What has been your greatest temptation and familiar spirit attack from your past? This is important to identify.

_____
_____
_____
_____
_____

How can you protect yourself from that? It is good to recognize this and safeguard your life from falling into the same traps.

_____
_____
_____
_____
_____

What are the "Must Haves" mentioned in this chapter that you know you should work on and pray about?

_____
_____
_____
_____
_____

What are the short-term and long-term goals that will help you live out your dream from God?

_____
_____
_____
_____
_____
_____

Spend some time to envision reaching your dream. Ask the Lord, "What does Your dream for me look like?" Journal what you see, hear, and sense.

_____
_____
_____
_____
_____
_____

ADDITIONAL RESOURCES_

RECONCILIATION PRAYERS AND ACTIVATION:

FATHER GOD

"To the fatherless he is a father. To the widow he is a champion friend. To the lonely he makes them part of a family. To the prisoners he leads into prosperity until they sing for joy. This is our Holy God in his Holy Place! But for the rebels there is heartache and despair." (Psalm 68:5-6 TPT)

- God is Love (1 John 4:8)
- God is Holy (Isaiah 43:15)
- Ancient of Days (Daniel 7)
- Beginning and the End (Revelation 1:8)
- Creator (Genesis 1)
- Healer (Exodus 15:26)
- Defender (Deuteronomy 32:4)
- Light (1 John 1:5)
- Compassionate & Gracious, slow to anger, faithful (Exodus 34:5-7)
- The God who provides (Genesis 22:14)

- Defense, strength, salvation (Isaiah 12:2)
- The Rock (Isaiah 26:4)
- Most High (Psalm 83:18)
- Sovereign, greatness, strong hand (Deuteronomy 3:24)
- Consuming Fire, Jealous for us (Deuteronomy 4:24)
- Shield (Proverbs 30:5)
- Banner of Victory (Exodus 17:15)
- Peace (Judges 6:24)
- Wise (Romans 11:33-34)
- Counselor (Psalm 16:7)
- Everlasting Strength (Isaiah 26:4)
- God of Wonders (Psalm 40:5)

PRAY OUT LOUD:

Father God, I ask that You reveal the truth of who You are to me in a very tangible way. I want to know You as the Scriptures above reveal Your character. I choose to forgive my earthly father(s) for everything done in my life outside of Your original intention for fatherhood. I release my father(s) from everything owed to me. I break and renounce any lies that I learned through my relationship with my earthly father(s). I ask You to please remove any false beliefs that I have about You, due to bad memories and experiences with men who played a primary role of influence in my life. Thank You, Father God, that You are not like men. I ask You to heal my heart from any wounds. Renew my thoughts and my perspective of You. I repent for all sins that I've committed against You and for any ways that I've misrepresented You to others. Father God, what truths do You want to reveal to me? (Pause in His Presence. Watch, listen, sense.) Father God, what do You think about me? (Pause in His Presence. Watch, listen, sense.)

HOLY SPIRIT

- The Holy Spirit Empowers You (Acts 1:8)
- Gives Life (John 6:63)
- Your Counselor and Helper (John 14:26)
- Comforter (John 14:16; John 14:26; John 15:26)
- Teacher (John 14:26)
- Resurrection Power (Romans 8:11)
- Testifies of Jesus (John 15:26)
- Gives Supernatural Gifts (1 Corinthians 12:8-10; Romans 12:6-7)
- Strengthens and Encourages (Acts 9:31)
- Leads and Guides (Romans 8:14)
- Reveals Truth (John 16:13)
- Helps You in Your Weaknesses (Romans 8:26)
- Intercedes (Romans 8:26)
- Searches the Deep Things of God (1 Corinthians 2:10)
- Sanctifies (1 Corinthians 6:11)
- Reminds You of the Word (John 14:26)
- Edifies You (1 Corinthians 14:4)
- Builds You Up (Jude 1:20)
- Gives You Rest (Isaiah 28)
- Refreshes You (Acts 3:19-21)
- Convicts and Forbids (John 16:8; Acts 16:6-7)
- Love, Joy, Peace, Patience, Kindness, Goodness, Faithfulness, Gentleness, Self-Control (Galatians 5:22-23)
- Hovered Over the Waters of the Earth During Creation (Genesis 1:1-2)
- Took Part in the Conception of Jesus within a Virgin (Matthew 1:18)
- Present During the Baptism of Jesus (Matthew 3:16)
- Present During the Resurrection of Jesus (Romans 8:11)

PRAY OUT LOUD:

Holy Spirit, I invite You to come. I want to experience the reality of who You are. I desire to know You personally. I choose to forgive everyone in my life that failed to comfort me, nurture me, and counsel me in a godly way. I release them from everything they owe to me. I ask You to fill every void in me, where these things have been missing. I break and renounce any lies that I learned through trauma, emotional pain, or sin. Holy Spirit, I ask You to heal my heart from any wounds. I ask You to please remove any false perspectives that I have about You. Remove all false doctrines or theologies I've learned about You. I repent for all sins that I've committed against You and for any ways that I've misrepresented You to others. Holy Spirit, what truths do You want to reveal to me? (Pause in His Presence. Watch, listen, sense.) Holy Spirit, I ask You to refresh me, saturate me, and fill me. (Pause in His Presence. Watch, listen, sense.)

JESUS

- Son of God (1 John 4:15)
- Savior (Acts 4:12)
- Light of the World (John 8:12)
- The Word of God (John 1:14)
- Truth (John 8:32)
- Redeemer (Job 19:25)
- Our Hope (1 Timothy 1:1)
- Friend (John 15:15)
- Chief Cornerstone (Psalm 118:22)
- Advocate (1 John 2:1)
- Mediator (1 Timothy 2:5)
- Faithful and True (Rev. 19:11)
- Good Shepherd (John 10:11)
- Holy Servant (Acts 4:29-30)

- King of Kings (Revelation 17:14)
- The One who Sets You Free (John 8:36)
- Author and Perfecter of Our Faith (Hebrews 12:2)
- The One Who Gives Eternal Life (John 10:28-30)
- By His Wounds We are Healed (Isaiah 53:5)
- Our Victory (1 Corinthians 15:57)
- Meets our Needs (Philippians 4:9)
- Offering and Sacrifice to God (Ephesians 5:2)
- Prince of Peace (Isaiah 9:6)
- Immanuel "God with Us" (Isaiah 7:14)
- The Way, The Truth, The Life (John 14:6)
- The Door (John 10:9)
- Resurrection and the Life (John 11:25)
- The One with All Authority (Matthew 28:18)
- Lion of the Tribe of Judah (Revelation 5:5)
- Indescribable Gift (2 Corinthians 9:15)
- Husband Bridegroom (Matthew 9:15)

PRAY OUT LOUD:

Lord Jesus, I invite You to come into every place of my soul and life. I ask that You reveal the truth of who You are to me. Jesus, I want to know You in the closest way possible. I ask for Holy Throne Room encounters with You. Come and do whatever You want to do in me. Jesus, give me more hunger for You and bless me with a grace to be consistent in prayer. Jesus, I ask for childlike faith so that I can explore who You are and Your Kingdom with awe, wonder, and adventure. I break and renounce any lies that I learned about You. I ask You to please remove any false perspectives that I have about You. Remove all false doctrines or theologies I've learned about You. I repent for all sins that I've committed against You and for any ways that I've misrepresented You to others in the past. Jesus, what truths do You want to reveal to me? (Pause in His Presence. Watch, listen, sense.)

Jesus, what new facet of Yourself do You want to reveal to me in this season of my life? (Pause in His Presence. Watch, listen, sense.) I declare that I am joined forever to the Lord and I am one spirit with Him (1 Corinthians 6:17). Amen.

HEALING MIRACLE DECLARATIONS

"But he was pierced for our rebellion, crushed for our sins. He was beaten so we could be whole. He was whipped so we could be healed." (Isaiah 53:5)

"He personally carried our sins in his body on the cross so that we can be dead to sin and live for what is right. By his wounds you are healed." (1 Peter 2:24)

- By Your stripes, Jesus, I am healed. Thank You for paying the price for my healing. (Isaiah 53:5)
- The healing of the Lord will spring forth speedily. (Isaiah 58:8)
- I cried out to You, God, and You healed me. (Psalms 30:2-3)
- God, I call on You in my day of trouble and I know You will deliver me. I glorify You. (Psalm 50:15)
- My healing has already been provided in the atonement. (Matthew 8:17)
- You will take sickness away from me (Exodus 23:20-25; Deuteronomy 7:12-15)
- Father God, Your Word is life to me and health to all my flesh. (Proverbs 4:22)
- According to my own faith, I am healed. (Matthew 9:22, 29)
- I praise You, Lord, and forget not all of Your benefits, that You forgive all of my sins and heal all of my diseases. Thank You for redeeming my life from the

pit and crowning me with love and compassion. (Psalm 103:2-4)
- I have been given a spirit of power, love, and a sound mind. (2 Timothy 1:7)
- I am spiritually clean. My old self has been removed. (Colossians 2:11)
- I am born again in Christ, and the evil one, the devil, cannot touch me. (1 John 5:18)
- No weapon formed against me shall prosper. (Isaiah 54:17)
- I can do all things through Christ who strengthens me. (Philippians 4:13)
- I have the Victory. (1 Corinthians 15:57)
- I am more than a Conqueror. (Romans 8:37)
- The weapons of my warfare are mighty through God. (2 Corinthians 10:4)
- Greater is He that's in me than he who is in the world. (1 John 4:4)
- The Lord is the strength of my life; Of whom shall I be afraid? (Psalm 27:1)
- When I speak the Word, it is quick, and powerful and sharper than a two-edged sword. (Hebrews 4:12)
- I am a Disciple of Jesus, so I have authority over every unclean spirit and all sickness and diseases. (Matthew 10:1; Mark 3:14-15; Mark 6:7; Luke 9:1)
- Father God, forgive me of all my sins. I choose to forgive and release everyone who has ever sinned against me. (Matthew 18:21-35, Matthew 6:9-13, Luke 5:17-26)

Additional Instruction for Healing in the Word of God:

Call for the elders of the church to pray for you, anoint you with oil, and lay hands on you for healing. (James 5:14; Mark 16:18)

Confess your faults one to another and pray for each other that ye may be healed. (James 5:16)

Understand the healing that comes through taking Communion. (1 Corinthians 11:27-30)

Repent from all sin in your life and go and sin no more. Sin is sometimes related to sickness. (Mark 2:5)

Forgive those who have sinned against you. Sometimes unforgiveness keeps us imprisoned. (Matthew 18:21-35)

SPIRITUAL WARFARE DECLARATIONS

- I am a new person. My past in forgiven and everything is new. (2 Corinthians 5:17)
- I am a child of light and not darkness. (1 Thessalonians 5:5)
- The sinful person I used to be died with Christ, and sin no longer rules my life. (Romans 6:1-6)
- I am free from the punishment (condemnation) my sin deserves. (Romans 8:1)
- I have been given the mind of Christ. He gives me His wisdom to make right choices. (1 Corinthians 2:16)
- I may approach God with boldness, freedom, and confidence. (Ephesians 3:12)
- I have been rescued from the dark power of Satan's rule and have been brought into the kingdom of Christ. (Colossians 1:13)
- I have been forgiven of all of my sins and set free. The debt against me has been cancelled. (Colossians 1:14)
- I have been given a spirit of power, love, and a sound mind. (2 Timothy 1:7)

- I am born again in Christ, and the evil one, the devil, cannot touch me. (1 John 5:18)
- No weapon formed against me shall prosper. (Isaiah 54:17)
- I can do all things through Christ who strengthens me. (Philippians 4:13)
- I have the victory! (1 Corinthians 15:57)
- I am more than a conqueror. (Romans 8:37)
- The weapons of my warfare are mighty through God. (2 Corinthians 10:4)
- I am seated with Christ in heavenly realms. (Ephesians 2:6)
- Greater is He that's in me than he who is in the world. (1 John 4:4)
- The Lord is the strength of my life; Of whom shall I be afraid? (Psalm 27:1)
- When I speak the Word, it is quick, and powerful and sharper than a two-edged sword. (Hebrews 4:12)
- I am a disciple of Jesus, so I have authority over every unclean spirit and all sickness and diseases. (Matthew 10:1; Mark 3:14 15; Mark 6:7; Luke 9:1)

MEET THE AUTHOR_

SULA SKILES is a speaker, author and sex trafficking abolitionist with a prophetic calling to the nations. It is her joy to advance the Kingdom of God with the love & power of the Gospel. She ministers in faith to see Jesus miraculously heal many. She loves the Presence & Glory of the Lord and invites people into deeper intimacy with Jesus as the Bridegroom King. Sula pastors alongside her husband John Mark Skiles. Together they are Church Planters and started Impact Life Church in Destin, Florida in March of 2014. They are incredibly blessed to have two beautiful children.

DISCOVER MORE AT:

 sulaskiles.com
Instagram / **@SulaSkiles**
Facebook / **@1SulaSkiles**

www.ingramcontent.com/pod-product-compliance
Lightning Source LLC
Chambersburg PA
CBHW070426010526
44118CB00014B/1926